D1026175

"*I love Chapter 1: Dream 'Til You Get Light-Headed. When I was growing up in Pawtucket, RI I used to be reprimanded for dreaming. I was told, 'Follow all the rules,' 'Don't do what you want; do what you're supposed to do.' Well, I'm here to tell you that this book has resurrected the kid in me, and I'm going to make it stick!*"

JANN TURSI, MARKETING ADMINISTRATOR

"*When you find one day, that you're not quite sure how you got to where you are, this book will help you to get a new start. With steps and sections on careers, relationships, even spiritual health, it encourages you to explore what you really want out of life. As a midlifer, I found this book just about perfect.*"

STEPHAN CHRISTIANSEN, INVESTMENT EXECUTIVE

"*As I read 'Tickle' it really hit me that among other things, the author has a tremendous gift for making formidable tasks suddenly appear doable and manageable.*"

BILL LAWTON, NETWORK ENGINEER

"*This beautiful book is a great gift for family and friends. It is powerful, uplifting, and it challenges you to embrace renewal with commitment and a sense of adventure.*"

SUSAN ELKO, EDUCATION CONSULTANT

"*CREATE A LIFE THAT TICKLES YOUR SOUL has renewed my spirit.*"

DIXIE STUMPF, EXECUTIVE ASSISTANT

"*For readers of any age, in any phase, this soulful book stimulates and inspires. I couldn't put it down. Now, I plan to go back and reread each lovingly crafted section. My life has been enhanced by reading this book.*"

AMANDA SOLER, EDITOR, *W4*

"Her description of the journey to a second life with authenticity and passion is riveting."

"Whatever your age, this inspiring book will make your life more meaningful. You'll learn how to let go of habits that no longer work and develop habits that will support the life you want. CREATE A LIFE THAT TICKLES YOUR SOUL will enliven your spirit and put spring in your step."

"If you are on a journey to a more meaningful life, this book is an informative, supportive guide."

"This heart-warming book offers insights that will enrich and even prolong your life. Expertly written by an author who clearly has 'walked her talk,' CREATE A LIFE THAT TICKLES YOUR SOUL invites you to open your heart, express your love, and live a life full of meaning and wonder."

"This book is stimulating as well as practical and full of great insights."

"This wonderful book already has helped me recreate parts of my life, and there are many inspirations waiting in the wings for more implementation. The ideas are so clear, relevant, and on target that I feel as if they were written directly to me."

"This book is having a positive impact on so many lives. It certainly touched mine."

HAPPINESS CAN BE BUILT
ONLY ON VIRTUE, AND
MUST OF NECESSITY HAVE TRUTH
FOR ITS FOUNDATION.

SAMUEL TAYLOR COLERIDGE

CREATE A LIFE *that* TICKLES YOUR SOUL™

Finding Peace, Passion, and Purpose

SUZANNE WILLIS ZOGLIO, PH.D.

TOWER HILL PRESS

Doylestown, Pennsylvania 18901

CREATE A LIFE THAT TICKLES YOUR SOUL is part of the
Tickle Your Soul™ series.

Paperback edition ISBN 0-941668-12-6
Copyright © 2000 by Suzanne Willis Zoglio, Ph.D.

Hardcover edition ISBN 0-941668-09-6
Copyright © 1999 by Suzanne Willis Zoglio, Ph.D.

Published by Tower Hill Press, Doylestown, PA 18901

Printed in the United States of America
Library of Congress number: 99-93719

A portion of the profits from this book is donated to charities.

In loving memory of Jill, Bill, Bob, and George

CONTENTS

ACKNOWLEDGMENTS

There are so many people to thank, not only for their contributions to this book, but to my personal learning and to the enhanced satisfaction of millions on progress journeys. I am most grateful for the guidance that so many authors have provided through their extensive research and inspiring writings, most especially to Gail Sheehy, Deepak Chopra, Jack Canfield, Stephen Covey, and Wayne Dyer.

Thank you also to the many people who so generously shared their midlife reinvention stories, thereby teaching and inspiring others who want to make their lives more meaningful.

And where would a writer be without both cheerleaders and constructive critics? Many, many thanks to Susan Elko, Ken White, Stephan Christiansen, Michael Stumpf, Lana Liberto, Lin Hodgdon, Doug and Carol Willis, Lou Manzi, and Louise Nugent for taking the time to review early drafts, providing encouraging comments and helpful guidance.

Many thanks to Alice Lawler, copyeditor and friend, for your sharp eye, tactful advice, and consistently positive support.

I am sincerely grateful to my sister Ann and brothers Doug, Lee, and David who have each loved, guided, and supported me over the years. I proudly look up to each of you and love you all.

Finally, loving gratitude to Mike, a constant source of love, strength, and nurturance. I could not have written this without your unwavering faith, essential guidance, and regular prodding.

Six years ago an executive client of mine was
being heavily recruited for one of the top positions in
a multinational firm. His salary and perks would have
been greatly enhanced, his influence would have grown
considerably, and the travel would have provided many
new adventures. It was a job offer that most people only
dream of. But, he told me point blank that he was not
going to accept the offer. If he were to accept the position,
he explained, he would have to move to Europe...and
uproot his family—his second family. He had reinvented
his family life just five years before and was determined
that this time around his family would come first.
"I know in my gut, it's just not a good fit for me," he
said. So, with wisdom and courage, he turned down
the offer...several times.

I was stunned by his decision...and greatly
inspired by his conviction to live a life that was right
for him. So inspired, in fact, that I set about reinventing
my own life. I began examining my mission, paying
more attention to my desires, and focusing more on
peace and passion than on accomplishments. I identified
life patterns that sometimes obstruct my path and committed to addressing those habits whenever they appear.
Throughout this book I will share my own experiences
along the road to reinvention in hopes that they might
support your journey.

When I first started to explore this phenomenon
of reinventing one's life, I cornered midlifers wherever
our paths would meet. We'd discuss changes they had
made or wanted to make in their lives. I would ask about

which aspects of life were most satisfying and which seemed out of sync. Many shared what they longed to embrace and which roadblocks were standing in their way. Each time I broached the subject, the response was the same. Eyes lit up in recognition, conversation exploded with examples of desired life changes, and a barrage of questions stormed passionately forward. "Are there really that many people who have successfully reinvented their lives? Why do so many 'midlifers' reinvent their lives? What makes some people quite content with their lives? How is it that some people have such passion for life? How do people find the courage to change? How do I go about creating a life that's right for me now?" And the parting question…"When will your book be ready?"

Over the last two years, I have surveyed, interviewed, and researched people in all walks of life—most in the second half of life—to answer those questions. In some of the case examples I have changed the names or identifying details to ensure privacy; some examples are composites. In all cases, I am sincerely grateful to those who have been generous enough to share their stories of how they managed to do what so many of us want to do at midlife…redesign our lives. Collectively, they demonstrate what can happen if you listen to your inner voice and then summon the courage to act from your heart.

As you are introduced to people who have refashioned their lives, you'll see that some have made significant changes in only one area, while others have overhauled their entire lives. They all are testimony to the resourcefulness of the human mind when guided by the human spirit. I hope their stories inspire you to create a life that's right for you…a life that tickles your soul.

If you are interested in leading a more satisfying life or in helping someone else to do so, this book provides more than inspiration; it provides practical guidance for creating a life that is right for you at this stage of your life. In the *Prologue* you'll find out what prompts people to make major changes in their lives and why it is especially common at midlife. You'll also learn about conditions that contribute to general satisfaction with one's life: authenticity, self-mastery, relationships, growth, and meaning. An absence of one or more of these conditions creates a yearning that motivates us to change. In Chapters One to Seven you will learn how to enhance these conditions by applying seven suggestions for successfully reinventing your life. You'll read how to find your purpose, change your mindsets, choose affirming behaviors, and attract both learning and love. You'll discover how to make the most of techniques such as reflective pausing, going to the balcony, visioning, goal-setting, reframing, solution sleuthing, and much more. You'll blast through old thought patterns to think anew, build your self-confidence, and find the courage to change whatever is no longer working for you. In the *Epilogue,* you'll be introduced to four stages of change that you are likely to experience as you make the journey from a life of reaction to one of deliberate action. You'll also learn how to generate the support you will need to break old habits and compose a new life based on the song in your heart.

I hope you decide to take this exciting journey into a world where you discover your own destination and make choices that serve your purpose well. You deserve much more than a "good" life. You deserve a life that is exquisitely tailored to the uniqueness of you. I wish you peace, passion, and purpose.

Bucks County, PA
March 21, 1999

suggestions for midlife pioneers

A STRONG MIDLIFE DESIRE
FOR PEACE, PASSION,
AND PURPOSE PROVIDES
THE MOMENTUM FOR
REINVENTING ONE'S LIFE.

S. W. Z.

PROLOGUE

suggestions for midlife pioneers

*h*ave you ever said to yourself or someone else: "I have *got* to get a life"? Or perhaps someone has told you that you really *should* get a life. "Getting a life" is a common goal for those of us past 40. We want to get it right for the next half of our lives. Some of us search for a way out of life's turbulence. Others want to feel more alive and savor the exquisite riches of life. And increasingly, we seek more meaning.

Well, if you are one of those people who want to get a life, I have good news and bad news. The good news is that there is every reason to believe that you *can* have the life of your dreams. The bad news is that you can't just *get* a life, as you would a quart of milk, a new stereo set, or a custom suit. You can't buy it, steal it, beg for it, or even trade for it. No one else knows what pictures fill your mind or what passions fuel your heart. You'll need to envision the design and embellish it with details that reflect the uniqueness of you. You will need to examine what feels right and what doesn't, what you should keep and what you should give away, what you should add and what would just clutter things up. The way to get a life that tickles your soul is to create it yourself. You will have plenty of company along the way.

Every eight seconds a baby boomer in America turns 50. We are the largest generation to enter midlife and we are entering a very different midlife from that experienced by our parents. Since an average 50-year-old today can expect to see an eightieth birthday, and many boomers are retiring earlier, the traditional "retirement" period of five to ten years is now likely to be longer and less retiring. According to Gail Sheehy, author of the groundbreaking book on adult life stages, *New Passages: Mapping Your Life Across Time,* we boomers have a whole "second adulthood," to look forward to before slowing down.

While some midlife reinventors get pushed head-first into the waves of change by illness, divorce, loss of a loved one, or being downsized out of a job, many of us willingly wade into uncharted waters in pursuit of something that's missing. We want to shift our lifestyles so they are more aligned with our inner needs and values. Situations that once seemed perfectly sensible and rewarding look quite different when viewed through the focusing lens of fortysomething.

In midlife, the need to accumulate material things becomes less significant than the need for time to enjoy what we have. The need for the approval of others becomes far less compelling than the need to follow dreams of our own. The need to be seen is superseded by the need to really see ourselves...and let others see that self too. As we assume positions of leadership in our careers and communities, we want to exercise that same level of influence in our personal lives as well. We become more insistent on living deliberately and according to our own rules. As we begin to lose parents, older siblings and even peers, we become keenly aware of our own mortality. Just as we hit our stride, time starts to really fly. Suddenly, we have an urge to do what we've always wanted to do...before it's too late. We want to taste life more fully, connect with others more honestly, and somehow have a hand in making the world a better place.

So we set out to reinvent our lives, seeking peace, passion, and purpose. For more peace we need to enhance authenticity and self-mastery (personal awareness and influence). For stronger passion we need to increase our zest for life through relationships and growth. For a sense of purpose we need to clarify what is meaningful to us. These five elements (authenticity, self-mastery, relation-ships, growth, and meaning) are associated with enhanced life satisfaction. When we have them we enjoy emotional well-being. When we don't have them we sense something is lacking. You'll be reading more about these five elements throughout the book, so let me provide a brief overview of each.

AUTHENTICITY: LIVING FROM THE INSIDE OUT

In the early stages of life we are focused on pleasing others (parents, teachers, bosses, spouses) in an effort to get our needs met. But as we mature, we are able to meet our own needs and are less motivated to do what others want us to do. We are weary of keeping up appearances, and care much less about what others might think. We no longer want to chase someone else's dream; we want to live our own. In short, we come to grips with the kind of person we have become and what it is we have achieved. Now we just want to live a life that *feels* right. We want to be free of inner turmoil and outer chaos. We look for more peace.

I suspect that you can probably name several people who have taken considerable risks in order to lead more authentic lives. Perhaps you know someone who has turned down a promotion to have more time with the family, forfeited a steady income to start up a new business, or left an unhappy marriage facing the firm disapproval of friends and family. Maybe you know someone who decided to start a family at 43, get a high school diploma at 52, or retire at 60 to work full time as a hospital volunteer. When you fashion a life where the decisions you make and the actions you take are considered, deliberate, and in harmony with what's important to you, you are living an authentic life. It is not necessarily a life that *others* admire or think is right for you, but a life that you know in your heart is right for you. It may not be a life that has been your habit, but it is a life that makes you greet each day with enthusiasm and sleep peacefully at night.

The more honest you can be (with yourself and with others) about who you are and what you need to be fulfilled, the more likely you are to create a life that's right for you. By aligning your outer behavior with your inner truth, life will flow in a direction that is meaningful to you. You will not expend energy on denial, survival, or suppression, but you will gain energy from insight, evolution, and expression...from being authentic. When your inner and outer worlds are congruent, the pieces all seem to fit...everything clicks. If you know at your core that you are living a life that is aligned with your purpose, filled with what you love, and supporting your growth, you are living an authentic life. Your outer behavior is fueled by your inner truth, and you lead a life of dignity and self-respect. There is no pretense to keep up. What you do reflects what you believe, how you feel, and what you know.

When you live authentically, you know what you stand for and make conscious choices. Your highest priorities consistently get the lion's share of your time, and your actions are consistent with your beliefs. If you say fitness, family, meditation, or service are important to you, you make time for them in your life. When you are complimented, you feel personally validated because it is the "real" you that is being appreciated, not a "persona" that you play very well. The energy that fuels an extraordinary life is harnessed from within your heart.

On the other hand, if you live in a way that just doesn't feel right, you might be concealing or ignoring parts of yourself that long to be acknowledged. Perhaps you feel tired, empty, or depressed because you are draining energy as you push your inner desires to the rear of your awareness. Denying inner truth is like trying to keep the lid on a pressure cooker that has built up too much steam. Try as you will, you can't contain it.

Being authentic often requires the courage to face personal truth. That truth might be how you really feel about yourself, what fears are blocking your success, which habits are perpetuating the life you have, or what dreams you have suppressed. Until you choose your actions based on inner knowledge and truth, you will not experience harmony. You may dance as fast as you can, distracting yourself from the inner work that needs to be done, but frenzied activity will not fill that void you perceive. To increase inner peace we must find the courage to live life from the inside out.

Enhancing authenticity in your life might add to your satisfaction if the statements below ring true for you.

• *You are skilled, perhaps very successful in your career, but not doing what you love.*

• *You don't know what you want, but know it's not the life you have.*

• *You want close relationships, but escape to work, food, or alcohol, instead of developing your own esteem and emotional aptitude.*

• *You know what changes would make your life more meaningful, but still find many excuses for not making the changes just now.*

If you related to any of the previous statements, give some thought to what would bring your inner and outer worlds into alignment. In Chapter One you will find out how to develop more direction from the inside out, and in Chapter Two you'll explore what habits might be keeping you from having the life that you desire.

SELF-MASTERY...BEING RESPONSIBLE AND COMPETENT

We all need to know that we are capable of surviving on our own. For high self-esteem and inner peace we must know at our core that we are "enough" just the way we are...and all by ourselves. We need to take responsibility for the choices we make and believe in our ability to handle whatever comes our way. If you can competently handle the basic details of life (e.g., shopping, cleaning, cooking, and banking), support yourself financially, manage time well, and deal with crises without falling apart, you probably have a strong sense of self-mastery. That doesn't mean that you *want* to be alone, but rather that you are not *afraid* to be alone.

You realize that events may occur outside of your control, but you can choose your response to those events. You take responsibility for the choices you make and for how you spend your time. Your days are not too rushed or overly complicated. Instead of feeling as though you are playing a bit part in someone else's movie, you feel as though you are producing, directing, and starring in your own masterpiece. You set achievable goals and reasonable schedules. You are able to say "no" to unreasonable requests and honor your own priorities. Because you do so, you find time for renewal and reflection and invest in relationships that are important to you. You make time to do what is fun for you and take responsibility for your own happiness.

People who have reached a high level of mastery often have a strong faith. They take responsibility for their actions and seek guidance through prayer or meditation. They are optimistic that all will work out for the best, so they act not out of fear, but out of intent. They go after what they want by taking risks and continuously improving their competence. With clear desires in mind and a belief that a power greater than their own will guide them, they move confidently toward the life they choose.

Also, since an accumulation of things can come at a high price for maintenance, "masters" often choose to simplify life by lessening their attachment to *things*...all of the must-haves that blur our vision, constrict our hearts, and gnaw away at our precious time. Serenity is more probable when we can distinguish what we really desire from what we habitually seek.

When you become a master of your own fate, a river of calmness flows through your life. You don't panic when adversity strikes. You remember past successes and trust that you will work things out. After all, you are master of your own life. If, on the other hand, you feel overwhelmed by normal life duties, under-prepared to earn a living, unable to control your own time, or panicky when crises occur in your life, you probably do not feel like master of your own fate. You may feel like a "victim" and make decisions based on what you *have* to do, rather than making decisions based on what you *choose* to do.

As you start thinking about how you'd like to live in the second half of your life, consider where you would like to exert more influence. Would it be in use of your time, managing your emotions, maintaining fitness and health, or perhaps developing satisfying relationships? As you proceed through this book you'll explore techniques for enhancing your influence and gaining more of the peace you seek.

RELATIONSHIPS...LOVING AND TRANSCENDING SELF

Research indicates that connections outside of ourselves are fundamental to a happy, healthy life. We all seek a sense of belonging and a way to transcend our limited sphere in relationship to something grander. Of course, you don't need research to convince you of that fact...just look around you. Think of a few of the most vibrant people you know. Do they have significant others in their lives? Do they maintain close relationships with family and friends? Are they members of a community that cares about them? Do they have a strong faith? Do they minister to others? If they are happy folks, you probably answered "yes" to several of those questions. People who surround themselves with love radiate an inner confidence, a capacity for joy, and an unusual generosity.

Have you ever noticed how alive you feel when there is a spontaneous flow of love in your life? It's not the same as receiving approval for something you did or bartering for something you'll get back. Unconditional love is pure and simple. If you have given or received such generous love you will know what a warm feeling it brings you.

A dear friend of mine shared a poignant story about such a bond. When her great-grandmother passed on and her belongings were being dispersed among the daughters, my friend's grandmother asked for only one thing. She wanted the fur coat that her mother had worn. "That way," she said, "whenever I wear it, I will feel her

loving arms wrapped around me." We are most alive...
most free to be the best we can be...when the fabric of our
lives is woven from threads of the heart.

Feeling loved and appreciated gives us an inner
richness that does not come from success or possessions.
Such "symbols" of love can do little to stave off the hollow
feeling of being alone. It takes bonds of caring with partners, friends, children, communities, or God to teach us
that we are lovable just the way we are. Then, we are able
to give generously from the heart and attract meaningful
relationships. In Chapter Five we'll explore ways of deepening many types of connections in your life.

GROWTH...CHOOSING CHANGE AND PROGRESS

Sometime in our late forties to early fifties we
make an important decision about the direction we'll
pursue for the second half of our lives. We either embrace
a spirit of renewal, growth, and adventure or we give in to
notions of settling in, slowing down, and taking it easy.
The decision is an important one since baby boomers
turning 50 today can look forward to another 20 to 30
active years and we are retiring earlier. While parents of
boomers generally retired near age 65 and used their
remaining five to ten years to "hit the rocking chair," the
landscape looks quite different for boomers whose retirement years might span ages 55 to 80 and beyond. That
would be a quite a long period of "rocking."

It has been said that there is no such thing as standing still. According to the laws of physics, living systems either grow or they begin to break down. This is true of the mind, body, and spirit. We stretch, learn, and expand or we shrink, forget, and contract. Think of how different older people can be. I have met alert and energetic 90-year-olds who bowl, swim and take college courses. I have also met frail 70-year-olds who don't even read the newspaper, let alone leave the house.

But, to seize growth opportunities we must move out of our comfort zones. And that takes courage and discipline. Alarms go off, and a myriad of questions appears. Do I still have what it takes to learn a new skill? Should I risk my retirement money to start a new business? Do I have the stamina to go mountain climbing? Is it too late to discover my spiritual self? Can I afford to spend my nest egg for tomorrow on what will please me today?

Each new adventure we face is like a double-edged sword. One side sparkles with the opportunity to grow and feed our passions. The other side casts a shadow of danger: we might get hurt, have to work too hard, or meet with public failure. If we retreat to the safety of what we know best and pass on the opportunity to experience growth we generally feel older, sensing that our world is turning in on itself. If we opt to feel the fear and do it anyway, we generally feel young and vital.

Before you paint a picture of the life you intend to have, consider what would rekindle the fire in your belly and increase your life energy by expanding your potential. You might think about what you have always wanted to do ...adventures that would quicken your pulse and enliven your soul.

MEANING...MAKING YOUR LIFE MATTER

When we are young our direction seems pretty clear. We go to school, get a job, find a partner, then get a better job. But later in life, our direction seems less clear. Starting in our late forties and intensifying through retirement, we begin to search for more meaning. Since we no longer need to blindly follow the path that pleases our parents or gains acceptance from our peers, we experience something that feels like an identity crisis. Except this crisis is not about individuation where we might ask, "Who am I?" This crisis is one of meaning. We ask questions like: "What's it all about?" "Am I contributing in any way?" "Am I reaching my potential?" We reflect on individual purpose, consider how we can contribute, look for self-understanding and growth, and seek connections outside of ourselves...often with nature, God, or our higher selves. We hit a stage of development when making money is not enough, having material things is fun, but not satisfying, and playing by other people's rules is really frustrating. As we come to grips with our own mortality, we look for all the ways that we can make the most of our potential, feel more in touch with the universe, and make a contribution.

A sense of purpose is so important at midlife that it is now commonplace to hear of people in their mid-forties to early fifties making major life changes. As we baby boomers march into our second adulthood we are changing careers, becoming full-time volunteers, writing books, adopting children, running for public office, becoming leaders at church, or otherwise reinventing our lives to include meaningful activity that goes beyond "earning a paycheck."

In the next seven chapters we will explore what you can do to enhance these five life-affirming conditions in order to find more peace, passion, and purpose. Each chapter focuses on one of seven suggestions for reinventing your life in such a way that soon you will be able to say that you have a life that tickles your soul.

Suggestions for Reinventing Your Life

1. Dream 'til you get light-headed...*feel the rush of clear vision and strong desire.*

2. Take responsibility for your present... *look back to the future.*

3. Create "tenant" rules for thoughts in your mind...*if they don't behave, evict 'em.*

4. Take your passions for a walk every day...*enjoy, embrace, and celebrate.*

5. Build bridges without tolls...*create relationships of caring and trust.*

6. Stretch until you feel it...*move out of your comfort zone to realize your potential.*

7. Make a difference every day...*change the world one act at a time.* ⇌

CHAPTER *1*

dream 'til you get light-headed

feel the rush of clear
vision and strong desire

A GREAT LIFE IS BORN

IN THE SOUL,

GROWN IN THE MIND,

AND LIVED FROM THE HEART.

S. W. Z.

CHAPTER *1*

*dream 'til you
     get light-headed*

 $\mathcal{A}$ great life is born in the
soul, grown in the mind, and lived from the heart. People
who are happiest in life seem to have mastered the art of
living from the inside out. Instead of living as others think
they should or as they are in the habit of living, they live
a life that *feels* right. They passionately pursue what they
are drawn to do, envision what they intend to accomplish,
and live the life of their dreams. These are the people we
envy because they seem so focused and so good at what
they do. It's as though they know a secret to living a fulfilling life...and they do. The secret is that a perfect life
begins with a dream. In the words of Roberta Hunter, the
late great jazz singer: "Honey, if you can dream it, you can
be it." And the dream begins from within...with a reflection on what it is that you were meant to do and what it
is that you desire.

CLARIFY YOUR PURPOSE

If you are spiritually oriented, you may have already explored this issue. According to Eastern philosophy, we all have a dharma or purpose in life—something that is uniquely suited to the talent we have been given. If you love what you do and you are using your unique gifts to make the world a better place, you are already serving your purpose. If you just don't feel right about what you do, probably you are not yet serving your purpose.

Not long ago I was facilitating a team development meeting with the senior executives of a government defense contractor. In doing the pre-retreat interviews, I found that one member of the team was especially appreciated...a real contributor in each team member's eyes. To my surprise, this great performer was planning his exit from the team. Although all appeared to be going well, he told me that while he was good at what he did and liked the people with whom he worked, he couldn't reconcile his values with the mission of the industry. He had been a pacifist for years, passionately embracing principles of nonviolence. He said that at first it was hard to admit this misfit, even to himself. After all, his job was secure, he earned a decent salary, and he was greatly respected by his peers. So, every day he'd push the nagging notions to the rear of his awareness, go to work, speak positively about the company, and then go home each night feeling a bit like a fake. Finally, in his mid-forties, he decided to listen to his inner voice. Actually he had never really felt right about working for a company in the business of "war," but the inner conflict was growing stronger and now he was more secure about making a change. The kids were grown, he had a decent nest egg, and his experience put him at an advantage in the job market. In fact, he had already received several unsolicited offers from technical companies outside of the defense industry. He knew it was time to leave the industry and relieve the inner dissonance that comes from living a life that doesn't feel right. He longed to be authentic and experience more inner peace.

Purpose and passion go hand in hand with a sense of inner peace. We all have heard many stories of people who changed the course of their lives by returning to an early passion that had been long neglected.

A young cellist became an engineer because his parents thought performers were a sorry lot. Years later, when he fell victim to a fatal disease and was given a short time to live, he returned to his lifelong passion of playing the cello. Miraculously, while performing for what he thought would be his last few months on earth, he recovered fully from the dreaded disease. He never returned to engineering, but embarked on a second career as a full-time concert cellist.

A former nun who left the convent to enter the business world rose from secretary to personnel manager to executive and finally CEO. After several years of leading the corporation, she resigned her position as bank president so she could once again lead a life of service...this time as head of a nonprofit agency. She earned a fraction of her corporate salary but added an immeasurable amount of meaning to her life.

When you apply your unique gifts to serve a need, you will be happy and uncommonly successful. That is the law of dharma, described most eloquently by Deepak Chopra, M.D., in *The Seven Spiritual Laws of Success: A Practical Guide to the Fulfillment of Your Dreams.* But how do you find out what you are predisposed to do? You can increase your awareness of your inner self and deepen your connections beyond yourself by regularly making time to reflect in silence. You can commune with nature more often to shed some of the chaos of your workaday world and expose more of your inner direction. Although you may not find the answers you seek immediately, you will begin peeling away the layers and seeing more of the light. To begin exploring your personal mission, you might try reflecting on these three questions:

1. *Do you love what you're doing so much that time flies and you feel exceptionally alive?*

2. *Are you presently expressing what you intuitively know are your positive personal traits?*

3. *Are you serving a human need...somehow making the world a better place?*

If you answered "yes" to those questions, you probably would describe your life as being meaningful and fulfilling. It is likely that you start each new day with focus, energy, and sheer delight.

If you answered "no," you might be feeling tired and burnt-out...as though you are working hard but not really accomplishing much worthwhile. Also, you might sense that you are not using a very special part of you. You may be skilled, even successful, but you do not feel a strong sense of purpose. Assuming you live well into your eighties, can you imagine retiring (in the traditional sense) for 30 years? It is more likely that you will pursue adventure, increase your learning, and be inspired to give something back. If you would like to explore your purpose further, complete any of the reflective exercises that follow.

Imagine Your Purpose as a Gift

———— ☙ ————

Before beginning this reflective exercise, which is adapted from the audiotape program entitled *Self-Esteem and Peak Performance* by Jack Canfield, find a quiet and private place. Sit silently, take a few deep breaths, and when you feel still, imagine that you are walking up a long path toward a beautiful light. As you near the light, you can see someone with arms outstretched offering you a box. Your purpose is inside. As you move closer, feel the warmth and love...notice the details of the box...its ribbon, color, and size. Accept the box gratefully, and then unwrap it. What do you see inside?

Whatever you see will be a symbol for your unique purpose. In one recent group a man explained that in his mental walk he received a book and that his purpose was to write. Someone else said she received a heart in her visual gift box and that she understood her purpose was to heal the world by teaching people to love. Another person found flowers and a kitten; her purpose is to nurture growth. If you do not see anything in your box, try the visualization again at another time when you are relaxed and still...perhaps just before you drift off to sleep at night. Keep a notepad by your bed to jot down any thoughts when you awaken, as they tend to disappear when your inner eye turns to the outer world of shower, shave, or traffic. If what you do visualize does not make any sense to you, don't worry. Write down what you see and later, perhaps when you least expect it, the meaning will become clear.

Match Your Gifts to a Human Need

When you apply your unique talents to meeting a human need, abundant wealth flows easily to you, according to Deepak Chopra's explanation of the law of least effort. It is the same principle that underlies the now-popular notion of "Do what you love and the money will follow."

To clarify your purpose, you might try listing your unique talents. List your unique positive traits...what you know is special about you and what others say when describing you. For instance, you might be described as insightful, imaginative, logical, artistic, engaging, witty, interesting, intuitive, warm, loving, strong, confident, trustworthy, persistent, convincing, inspiring, charismatic, expressive, peaceful, or collaborative. If you are not sure of your traits, ask several people who know you what they see as your dominant positive traits.

Now, pick the two or three traits that most clearly represent you and consider how you presently enjoy expressing those traits. How could you make a difference by expressing your gifts in those ways? For instance, if your traits are "witty" and "observant" and you enjoy telling stories about life's little dramas, you could inspire people to live more harmoniously through your work as a novelist, playwright, or even stand-up comedian. If you are "witty" and "observant" but enjoy expressing those traits through drawing, you might add humor to the world by developing cartoons, funny greeting cards, or humorous ad campaigns.

Just Ask the Question
───── ᴥ ─────

In *Stop Out-of-Control Eating* (a book that is founded on *A Course In Miracles*™), author Karen Anne Bentley suggests a straightforward approach to finding your purpose; she says we should just ask. Sitting quietly, relax with a few deep breaths and then when you are still and focused—all channels open, so to speak— simply pose this question: "What is your will for me?" You can direct your question to God, your higher self, the universe, or to whatever you recognize as the source of love and wisdom. If you don't immediately "hear" the direction of your purpose, develop a habit of sitting in silence every day for 15 to 30 minutes. Do nothing...just pose your question and listen.

Write from Your Inner Voice
───── ᴥ ─────

Try defining your life purpose by writing it out. Following a format similar to that offered below, just start writing. Don't labor or analyze; just let the words flow. Write several different statements until one captures your heart. Be patient; when you are ready, your purpose will reveal itself.

My Purpose Statement
———— ❧ ————

"I enjoy expressing my positive traits of

_____ and _____ by

doing _____

to help others _____

_____."

If you still are not clear about what it is that you are meant to do, consider leaving the question for a while and returning to the nature of your calling later. Or, if you feel motivated to continue the exploration, consider varying your approach a bit. You might take a meditative approach but ask a different question. Find a quiet place where you can reflect in silence. Settle in comfortably, take several deep breaths, and exhale slowly. Close your eyes, and when you feel stillness within, pose the question: *"How can I be of service to others?"* Just wait for an image, a sound, or a word to bubble up. If the message is not clear immediately, write it down anyway. Later you will see the meaning. If no answer comes, finish your meditation and move on. The response may pop into your head later.

To take a cognitive approach, sit down with pen and paper, and answer the following two questions.

1. *For what have I always had a natural inclination or talent (building, composing, analyzing, problem solving, risk taking, humor, selling, story telling, etc.)?*

2. *If I could improve just one thing in this world, what would it be?*

Putting those two things together may point you in a direction that will add meaning to your life. Remember Deepak Chopra's sage advice that when unique talent is applied to meeting some human need, the result will be uncommon and effortless wealth.

Not everyone that changes careers does so through an orderly sequence of reflective activities. Some midlifers just follow their intuition; they simply know that what they want to do is very different from what they have been doing. A recent *Wall Street Journal* article written by Kevin Helleker reported an interesting trend of an exodus from professional services into the land of fitness training. Describing midlife shifts of dentists, accountants, lawyers, and computer service professionals, the article recounted the power of the pull toward enhancing one's fitness, helping others, connecting more personally, and making a difference in the lives of others. It seems that many midlifers go into the gym as well-paid professionals in need of personal physical development and come out as fitness trainers with a passion for helping others stretch themselves.

One 47-year-old dentist explained that although he earned only one-third of his former salary, his clients appreciate him so much more than his patients ever did. Knowing that he is making a real difference by helping people to live longer and live more fully gives him intense focus. Another trainer—once a computer programmer and now a fitness trainer for the Indianapolis Colts cheerleaders—stated how he wakes up each day thinking how good it is "to be me." A 40-year-old Texas lawyer made light of not using his years of schooling by saying that he didn't want to throw good time after bad. Some people just know when their purpose presents itself and no logical reasoning can override their intuitive drive to do what they are called to do.

CREATE A VISION OF THE LIFE YOU WANT

When you have a sense of where you're going, you can begin fleshing out the details to create a vision of the life you want. Don't worry if you are not sure of what it is that you can do to make a difference—it will unfold for you later. In fact, some midlifers tell me that once they reflected on their "ideal life," their purpose became clear. When you are ready, begin creating a clear and compelling picture of the kind of life you'd like to have.

When I embarked on reinventing my life, I was 46 and probably seemed to have it all: a great husband, a successful consulting practice, two new books, leadership opportunities in our community, and a comfortable lifestyle. But it felt like something was missing. I questioned all aspects of my life, career, relationships, and sense of purpose. Those closest to me said I was going through a midlife crisis, and perhaps at that turning point it *was* a crisis. Today, it feels more like a journey. My direction is clearer, and every day I do more of what I love. My relationships are deeper, and I'm taking better care of myself. But I also know that there is no "end"...just higher plateaus. As Robert Frost wrote, "I have miles to go before I sleep...miles to go before I sleep." I'm still learning to accept without judging, follow my heart, and seek guidance from many sources.

As with any journey, the path to your better life begins with a clear destination and a particular route that you want to follow. Nothing is more inspiring than having a place you can't wait to get to and certain milestones that signal you are on the right path. So think of your purpose as the "country" of your destination. Then decide how much of the country you want to see, which parts you'll really want to explore in depth, what sites would be fun to see just once, how much you want to learn before you go...and so forth.

To begin creating your vision pretend it is one year from now, and you are writing a letter to a dear friend, describing your *new* soul-tickling life. What does it look like? You might begin by explaining how you are doing what you love to do and making a difference by doing so. Then add any life details that come to mind (i.e., where you are living, whose love you share, what you have learned, and how you enjoy life each day). Describe the life you want as if you were already living it. You might consider including one or more of the following details:

My efforts are focused on...

I generally feel...

I have relationships that are...

I'm in an environment that...

My finances are...

I'm making a difference by...

Physically, I am...

Spiritually, I am...

New adventures in my life include...

I find great joy in...

A dream life is founded on purpose, structured on core preferences, and embellished with personal desires. The more detailed your vision, the more likely you are to see it. When you have a few moments, focus on all that you desire. Know what it is that you want in your life, whether it is love, money, or specifics such as a house on a cliff overlooking the ocean. What is it that you intend to have in your reinvented life? Write these desires down and read your list often.

You now have a purpose, descriptions of how various aspects of your life will look, and a list of your deepest desires. Using what you identified in those three areas, you might want to formulate a vision statement of two or three lines that expresses the essence of the life you want to see. This is what you will be posting, reading, imagining, depicting, and symbolizing later. Here's one format that might get you started. Modify it any way you like to make it exquisitely yours.

My Intended Life

I am doing what I love: _____

_____

in _____.

My good life includes: _____

_____.

I'm feeling _____

and helping others to_____.

I am grateful for _____

_____.

Once you have created a vision statement that you love, print it (in beautiful calligraphy if that inspires you). Frame it, reduce it for your wallet, laminate it, or write it on Post-It® Notes and place it where you will see it several times every day (e.g., bathroom mirror, daily planner, dashboard of your car, refrigerator, or telephone).

GIVE YOUR ASPIRATIONS A PAIR OF HIKING BOOTS

Once you have a purpose that inspires and a dream of desires, you are ready to plan for the changes you want to see in your life. You are ready to transform your dream into reality by setting related goals and taking action. Without goals, you are at the whim of life's breezes. You may float, swirl, rise high or fall, but when the wind dies down, you haven't moved forward at all. Following your dream fuels your passion with a picture of your desired state and releases great energy from deep in your soul. Goals focus your energy and keep you on the path to your destination.

An action plan is like a progression of stepping stones that—if traversed—will take you into your dream. Remember: "If you continue to do what you've always done, you'll continue to get what you've always got." To have a different life, you've got to *do* things differently.

Using your vision that includes doing what you love, making a difference in the world, and having what you desire, try listing five to eight broad goals that—if achieved—would bring you closer to a life that tickles your soul. For example your list might include: increase my attention to nature, reflect in silence, attract more love, use my talents, and become physically fit.

"Based on my vision, my priority goals are…"

Now, to increase your chances of attaining your goals, break them into specific, measurable action objectives, each with its own time limit. Actions can be big or small, long-term or short-term. List any action that will move you closer to your goal. For instance, if "less stress" is one of your goals—How *did* I know?—your goal/objectives list might look something like the one that follows.

Sample Action Objectives List for a Goal of Less Stress
- Drink only two caffeine drinks per day.
- Sleep at least seven hours every weeknight.
- Listen to uplifting audio tapes weekly.
- Meditate for 30 minutes 3x per week.
- Exercise 30 minutes 3x per week.
- Work maximum of 50 hours per week.
- Delegate one administrative task a month.
- Work from home one day a week.

Perhaps it will help to think of a goal (e.g., higher self-esteem) as a desired outcome, and an objective (e.g., finish my degree this year) as a milestone along the way to that outcome. An objective is a behavior. Notice that each objective above begins with an action verb...something you can *do* to reach your goal of less stress. A goal is something you desire, something you want to *be or see* in your life. An objective is something you intend to do that will move you closer to your goal. Now, for each of your five to eight priority life goals, list several actions that you can take to move closer to that goal. Write as many as you like, and don't worry about form. Later, you can add time elements and make your action objectives more specific, if necessary. For now, just think of all you can do to give your aspirations a pair of hiking boots.

Once you've listed your objectives, check to see that each is measurable. You have probably heard the expression: "What gets measured, gets done." Well, that is true in your personal life as well as in your work life. Develop objectives that you can check off as accomplished when you are done. You should be able to say, "Yes, I did that." Succeeding with these milestones will maintain your energy and inspire you to keep going. When you see progress you will want to keep progressing. One way to stay apprised of your progress is to set action objectives, accomplish them, and check them off as "accomplished." To know *when* you have achieved each objective, add a time deadline. It will create a sense of urgency. You know how much you accomplish when you have a deadline, so set a deadline for each objective...a self-imposed deadline that will hold you accountable to yourself.

Once you have developed your action list, keep it visible. Post it, consult it at least daily, and check off items as you complete them. It will spur you on to see your successes in black and white. Add new steps when your list has dwindled, and regularly check unattained goals to see if they are still important. If not, cross them off. I like to type my purpose, vision, and values (which don't change very frequently) all on one page, and my priority goals and action objectives on a second, since it is a living document, changing day to day. Determine what would work best for you. Some people transfer short-term objectives to their weekly planner. It's a good way to make sure that you are acting on your goals every day.

Since at some time in our lives, most of us have set goals that we didn't attain, it's probably a good idea to consider what motivates us to achieve our goals. As mentioned, action objectives should be specific, measurable, and include a time element. In addition, according to expectancy theory of motivation, you are more likely to achieve your goals if you expect two things. For highest motivation, you must believe that your goals are attainable and that they will result in a reward that you desire.

Let's consider the second condition first. See if your goals are related to something that is really important to you. In other words, are these goals that you choose to set for yourself, not that someone else is setting for you? One way to determine the relevance of your goals is to ask yourself why you want to accomplish them. How will you feel when you do accomplish them? If your answers relate to *extrinsic* rewards (i.e., pleasing others, getting approval) you will not be passionate about succeeding and if you do, any victory will be a hollow victory. You will not feel any joy or sense of accomplishment. If, on the other hand, your answers relate to *intrinsic* rewards (i.e., to do what you know is right, to help you fulfill your purpose, to receive what you really desire) the results will be meaningful to you.

Now, let's consider the condition of attainability. This is a little like the chicken and the egg—which comes first? Do you set goals that are obviously attainable, or do you increase your belief in yourself so lofty goals appear doable? I believe the answer is "both." Set lots of goals within a wide range of difficulty—some you can accomplish tomorrow and some that you consider "shooting for the stars." At the same time, reflect, meditate, and focus on your intent to strengthen your belief that you can be, do, and have anything you wish. In the next chapter we will explore what you can do to maintain such a positive belief system and thereby increase the probability of realizing your dream. ⤳

Into Your Dream

Some stepping stones to dreams are small,
Others are large and slick.
Some have rough and ragged edges,
For your weary feet to grip.

Some are spaced so far apart
Your legs will hardly reach.
Others nest atop each other,
Like pebbles on a beach.

For some you'll need to leap with faith.
On others, move with balance.
A few will take uncommon grace.
For most…your skill and talent.

You know the way, so just begin.
Then keep a steady pace.
Stretch and rest…and soon you'll see
You've reached your special place.

S. W. Z.

CHAPTER *2*

---

take responsibility
for your present

look back
to the future

TO TAKE RESPONSIBILITY FOR
A FULFILLING LIFE
IS TO CHOOSE HOW YOU USE
EACH DAY OF LIFE.

S. W. Z.

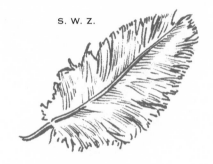

CHAPTER *2*

---

take responsibility for your present

*T*aking responsibility for your happiness means making deliberate choices about how you respond to your past, present, and future. You can bury your past and let unconscious self-defeating habits sabotage the life you want or you can choose to explore your past and change any negative patterns that are getting in your way. You can assume a victim's stance in your present life or you can choose to take charge of your life and create whatever circumstances you need. You can walk blindly into your future with little sense of where you're headed, or you can choose to design an incredible future and act in alignment with that intent. The choices are yours.

OLD HABITS CAN SABOTAGE SUCCESS

If you are going to reinvent your life it will help to take a look at any patterns in your life today that regularly seem to get in the way of you creating the life that you want. If you can understand the origins of such behaviors, you will have a good chance of changing them. A clear direction and a list of goals can only guide you to success if you are aware of which behaviors support your growth and which will effectively block any progress. This chapter will help you to identify any old patterns, unhealthy guilt, or negative self-talk that might be sabotaging your success.

Let me share a personal learning. For much of my life I have been a fiercely independent overachiever and an inveterate helper. Growing up in an environment where I was left to assume responsibility for others and myself at a very early age, I developed coping patterns that worked well back then and—to some degree—helped me to succeed in early adulthood. Because of such drive I have completed graduate programs, written books, earned a good income, and made a difference in many lives. However, at their most dominant, those childhood scripts of "needing to do more," "doing it all on my own," and "keeping everyone else happy" would set me adrift in waters well over my head. So, although I wanted to have more time to write and live a more balanced life, my old life patterns were sabotaging my success. Always wanting to help resulted in far too many commitments. Doing everything just right—and all by myself—made handling all of those commitments a rather tricky proposition.

I had to learn to focus on what is meaningful, set reasonable limits on my time, take care of my own needs, and ask for help when I need it. If I remember to do so—tolerating whatever shadows of guilt and discomfort still linger—I am more productive and I experience more joy and inner peace.

Before designing a life that feels right from the inside out, it will help to get better acquainted with the inner you. You'll need to set aside some time to reflect on what makes you "tick" and what would make your life really "click." With such sharpened awareness of any habits that are getting in the way of you having what you want, you'll be better prepared to direct your energy in constructive ways. You'll blast through obstacles and start living the life of your dreams.

Getting a different life usually means thinking and behaving differently. While it may sound overly simple, it is true that if you continue to do what you have always done, you'll continue to get what you've always got. So if you want a different life, you've got to stop doing what isn't working and establish new patterns of behavior. But old habits are hard to change even when we are aware of them. If we're *unaware* of them, they're impossible to change. The first step in fashioning a new life is to raise your awareness of life patterns that might be blocking you from creating the life of your dreams. Remember, however, that you can't drive forward while looking in a rear view mirror. So check what's back there and then focus on your future intent.

As children we were loved, guided, and protected by others in varying degrees. Based on those early experiences, we adopted certain mindsets about our own self-worth and how the world operates. Although many of the "lessons" we learned as children do not make any sense when examined against the backdrop of our adult lives, we often continue to operate under false beliefs just out of habit. The only way to change them is to take stock of how many are lurking around and consciously decide to address each one.

See if any of the following beliefs, behaviors, and early circumstances are familiar to you. If they are, you can choose to deal with them now and consciously commit to breaking any negative habits that stem from them. You can give up any beliefs that are no longer true and stop sabotaging your quest for peace, passion, or purpose.

> *Putting roadblocks in the way of getting the love you want.* For instance, do you set yourself up for failure by engaging in relationships with people who are unstable, unreliable, or emotionally unavailable to you? Or if you do find someone trustworthy, do you become so possessive that you drive the person away (making your

worst fear of abandonment a reality)? Maybe you hold back in relationships in order to avoid intimacy. If so, it is possible that when you were young, you lost a parent to illness, death, or divorce or that you grew up with caretakers who provided inconsistent love. But it is not too late to change the impact of those early days. You can learn to behave in a way that will attract people you can count on and attract the love you want.

Seeing yourself primarily as a victim to whom bad things always happen. For example, do you generally resign yourself to whatever life dishes out? Do you normally try to please, but sometimes lash out at others with put-downs, sarcasm, or anger? Possibly, people who want to soothe you and love you feel frustrated because for you "enough is never enough." Do you overindulge in work, food, alcohol, or taking care of others, but fail to take care of yourself? Perhaps earlier in life someone hurt you or you observed someone else being hurt. Today, you can protect yourself by strengthening your sense of self-worth and learning to love yourself just the way you are.

Feeling lonely, disconnected, or cheated out of something in life. Can you sometimes be resentful, demanding, and cynical? Perhaps you react to gestures of kindness as if you expect them. If so, it's possible that you did not receive much nurturing, empathy, or guidance as a child. But as an adult you can decide to release your anger at not having your needs met and retrain yourself to give and attract more love.

Attaching yourself to others who will take care of you. Do you often feel overwhelmed by life's daily chores, finding normal working, cooking, cleaning, and finances hard to handle without help? Perhaps you wish for more support than you get or have many "back-up" supporters who rush in to help whenever you send out an SOS? If so, it is possible that you were overprotected as a child with someone handling so many things for you that you never learned that you are capable of coping on your own. Or perhaps you were underprotected as a child and have always felt "in over my head." If so, you can learn to recognize your successes and capabilities, develop new competencies, and enhance your confidence to handle life more on your own.

Finding yourself overscheduled, overworked, and near exhaustion. Is it difficult for you to ask for and even to receive help? Does everything need to be done your way? You might make it difficult for others to help you by not stating what you need or by making the standards so high no one else can help. Perhaps you were on your own too early as a child, assuming responsibility beyond your years. If so, you can learn to shift your mindset to one of healthy interdependence. You can learn how to ask for and graciously receive what you want.

Avoiding risks that are necessary for you to actualize your dreams. Are you generally unsure of yourself, especially when it comes to making decisions that could have important consequences? Do you feel like a bit of a failure or a successful "fraud?" If so, you might have been overly criticized or unfavorably compared to others when you were young Perhaps you failed in school or at sports. If so, it's not too late to embrace empowering thoughts and build your risk-taking repertoire. You can learn to leave the comfort of the known in anticipation of the exhilaration that comes with reaching new plateaus of your potential.

Since a majority of us grew up in families where our needs were not fully met, it is quite possible that your early life did not provide you with a strong sense of self-worth and confidence in your ability to cope. According to Dr. Charles L. Whitfield, author of *Healing the Child Within*, between 80 and 95 percent of us grew up in dysfunctional families. Before you can create a new life for yourself it is important to examine your early beginnings so you can see if any leftover anger, hurt, or mistaken beliefs are getting in the way of the life you want.

If you would like to learn more about negative life patterns and how they could be sabotaging your personal happiness, consider reading *Reinventing Your Life*, an insightful book by cognitive therapists Jeffrey E. Young, Ph.D. and Janet S. Klosko, Ph.D. You might also consider working with a counseling professional. As you proceed through the rest of this book you will learn several ways to turn self-defeating behaviors into life-affirming actions.

WHAT'S THAT WEIGHING YOU DOWN?

As children, we do whatever it takes to protect ourselves and get approval or love. Depending on the reaction our behaviors elicit, we soon categorize behaviors as either "good" (those that get attention, approval, and love) or "bad" (those that prompt rejection, humiliation, or anger). So if we are punished or rejected when we are expressing feelings, having fun, or speaking up, we stuff those "bad" parts of ourselves into a secret suitcase which becomes a repository for our shame, guilt, resentments, mistakes, and hurts. We may unconsciously drag that baggage around for the rest of our lives. Occasionally, we may recognize faint voices from the suitcase, crying to come back into our lives. More often, we experience a vague sense that something is missing and to be whole we need to reclaim something of value that was stashed away a long time ago.

Most of us need to heal, forgive, and reclaim some of the energy it takes to lug around that bag stuffed with parts of ourselves that we need to acknowledge and reattach. The parts that you need to reclaim might be ones that you perceive as "positive" (most likely those that you strongly admire in others) or "negative" (most likely traits that you vehemently despise in others). In truth there is no such split. You are all of your traits and you are lovable just as you are. You may choose to learn and grow and evolve, but there is no "bad" you that you need to stuff away. Perhaps you need to reclaim the courage you used to have to seek adventure, the curiosity for learning that once excited you, the unbridled passion of your sexuality, or your ability to spontaneously ask for what you want. Once you can acknowledge and accept all parts of you without judging any part, you will free up tremendous energy that will help you to grow. If you can reclaim the parts that you have stuffed away, your burden will be lighter, and you will be able to move forward with greater ease and speed.

Joan Borysenko, Ph.D.—cellular biologist, psychotherapist, and co-founder of the Mind/Body Clinic, New England Deaconess Hospital—is the author of *Guilt Is the Teacher, Love Is the Lesson*. In that book, she describes 21 signs that indicate we may have stuffed important parts of ourselves away at an early age. Some of the signs include: being overbusy, taking on too many commitments, being a compulsive helper, not being able to say no, constantly apologizing, blaming ourselves for everything that goes wrong, being overly sensitive to criticism, not being able to ask for help, worrying we're not good enough, worrying about illness, being a perfectionist, and trying to control everything and everyone.

When I first read that list, I checked off more than half of them. Today, I still struggle with a few, but I'm making progress. More frequently I say "no" to requests that don't fit into my priorities and ask for what I want. I don't attempt to control situations as much and I'm learning to relax my expectations of others and myself. If any of the above behaviors sound familiar to you, as they did for me, gently acknowledge them as yours, but try not to criticize yourself. Remember that we've been lugging these suitcases around for a long time. We're not going to relinquish them overnight.

The first step in any change process is awareness. If we can recognize self-defeating behaviors (e.g., doing too much, always needing to be right, projecting our perceived "flaws" onto others, or blaming others for our own unhappiness), we have a good shot at changing them.

LIGHTEN UP BY LETTING GO

In a lecture from his audiotape series, *Self-Esteem and Peak Performance*, Jack Canfield asks his live audience how many people have some resentment toward their parents for not meeting all of their needs when they were young. Most raise a hand. Then he asks, "How many of you who raised your hand clearly asked your parents for what you wanted?" No hands go up. His third question, "How many of you had professional psychics for parents?" prompts much laughter of recognition. His main point becomes perfectly clear: it is easier to forgive our parents for not giving us all that we needed, if we can recognize that they behaved according to what they knew at the time. If we can't understand and forgive, the baggage can slow down the journey into our dreams. This was the case with Jim until he became aware of the weight and repacked his baggage.

When Jim speaks about his parents, he describes them as aloof and critical. He says that nothing he did was ever right and he can't remember receiving much warmth or affection. After college he married someone who was non-critical but who also was not very expressive. His wife was a loyal spouse, but not emotionally available. Jim's life pattern had drawn him into a love relationship that was remarkably similar to the one he had with his parents—one of detachment.

Like many men in midlife, Jim was becoming increasingly aware of his need to feel a deep connection. He realized that only love and affection could fill the hole he felt inside. At first, he tried to be more loving and expressive himself; then he tried to get his spouse to be more loving and affectionate. Finally, he left the marriage, in search of something more.

He dated, even bonded in a few important relationships, but it finally became clear—after a few counseling sessions—that the problem was too much baggage. He realized that unless he let go of the anger and resentment that he still felt toward his parents for depriving him of the nurturing that he needed as a child, he would not be able to love himself or anyone else deeply. He was hanging on to the anger so tightly, that he was literally cutting off the circulation of love.

Jim did some cathartic letting go under the guidance of his therapist and he became quite a student of material on enhancing self-esteem. He is now in a healthy relationship and says that he is learning to express love more openly and be more open to receiving it as well.

If you have trouble forgiving someone for causing you pain, you might try this technique before you go to sleep tonight.

Campfire of Forgiveness

Just before you go to sleep, relax with some deep breathing (inhale slowly to the count of eight, hold four counts, and exhale slowly to the count of eight; repeat three or four times). When you are relaxed, visualize a campfire with roaring flames. Picture around the campfire anyone that has hurt you or anyone you have hurt.

Walk with one person at a time to the campfire, carrying a heavy log between you. As you get to the fire, toss the log of your mutual grievances onto the flame. Join hands with your forgiveness partner as you watch the flames consume your anger, pain, regret, and shame. Feel the fire melting any tension between you and forging a new bond of trust. When you are ready, separate, and join another person in the walk to the fire.

Continue the process until all the people
you have "invited" have walked with you.
Now, rest peacefully with a clear mind and
a loving heart.

It is possible that you do not want to forgive those
who have wronged you. In that case, at least try to lighten
your baggage a bit by acknowledging your feelings and
expressing your anger. If it is unwise, uncomfortable, or
impossible to confront the person directly, you can write
a letter explaining how that person's behavior made you
feel. You don't even have to mail the letter; many people
find that the act of writing itself is enough for them to let
go of some of the anger and move on. If your memories
were particularly painful, you probably would benefit
from the support of a counseling professional who can
guide you through the process of releasing strong feelings
and allowing old wounds to heal.

The same principle of forgiving others applies to
self-forgiveness. Whenever you behave in a way that you
later regret, try to remember that we all act according to
our capability at the time. We all have regrets...times
when we're consumed with thoughts such as, "I wish I had
not broken that confidence," "I'm sorry I let her down,"
or "If only I hadn't said that." Also, we all make mistakes...work errors, social faux pas, bad investments, and
impulsive decisions. But we can learn to see them for

what they are: blips, missteps, mind-pops, or soul-lapses. We can learn to admit when we are wrong, apologize to others when we hurt them, and forgive ourselves for not being perfect. We can become more accepting of our imperfections and in doing so become more authentic and whole. We can learn to view our mistakes as lessons in the school of life. Rationally, you know that one trait or one mistake does not a "bad" person make. So lighten up a bit, and give yourself and others a little slack.

BE SELF-DIRECTED

It is so easy to look at the lives of those around us and wish we had it so good. Maybe it's the money, the great job, or those terrific kids that we envy. Maybe it's the good looks, excellent health, or unshakable faith. Whatever it is, other people often seem to have it easier. Hence the expression: "The grass is always greener on the other side." Not long ago, I came across a variation of that expression on an Internet site (Hard@Work.com). M.D. Clark, a visitor to the site, sent in this twist: "The grass may be greener on the other side, but it's just as hard to mow."

When we are longing after someone else's life, we need to remember that every result is the consequence of an action. If you envy the wealth of a sibling, do you also envy the 18-hour work days and 21 days per month of travel abroad? When you are thinking how great it would be to look as fit as your coworker down the hall, are you also thinking of how great it would be to work out at 5:30 every morning and maintain a low-fat diet? When you dream of being as peaceful as your neighbor, do you also dream of meditating for 30 minutes twice a day, every day? If not, you're only seeing half of the picture—the end result without the action that precipitated the result.

What we get out of life is usually in direct proportion to the choices we make and the actions we take. We have to assume responsibility for imagining what we want in our lives, and then choosing our responses to people and situations according to our intended objective. In the words of Stephen Covey, author of *The 7 Habits of Highly Effective People*, if we want to succeed in life, we must become "response-able."

Being "response-able" means that you increase your ability to respond—not react—to situations, people, and circumstances. Between the stimulus (someone insults you) and the response (your behavior), there is the element of choice. You can choose to insult back, ignore the insult, or take offense. The choice is yours. You don't have to react—as an animal might in either fleeing or fighting. Instead, you can deliberately choose which response to the situation is the right response. What is the difference between "reactive" and "response-able"? Let me give you a few examples.

Imagine a pair of 45-year-old twins. Both lose their management jobs at exactly the same time due to corporate downsizing. Twin A begins grumbling at the first hint of the layoffs and is still cursing the unfairness of the severance six months later...to his comrades in the unemployment line. Twin B begins getting his resume together at the first hint of the layoffs and is found learning a new computer system six months later...with his new coworkers.

The situation is the same for both twins (a job layoff), but their responses are quite different. Without much forethought, Twin A *reacts* to the situation, while Twin B accepts responsibility for his future and makes some deliberate choices. First, he proactively polishes his resume, and then he invests energy in job hunting instead of badmouthing senior management. Finally, he takes a few risks (learning new skills and developing new relationships) that will help him improve his situation. In other words, Twin B takes charge of his own future, instead of letting the situation dominate.

Consider another example. Two women in their late forties both find out that their husbands have been unfaithful. After several attempts to patch things up, both women offer their husbands the same ultimatum: "End the affair and recommit to our marriage, or move out." Surprisingly, both husbands leave. Both wives are devastated, but they respond differently. Julia, woman #1, goes through a normal cycle of denial, anger, hurt, and acceptance. She seeks support from a therapist, applies to a graduate program, lands a top position at a prestigious institution, and eventually begins dating again. Sarah, woman #2, becomes nastier by the day, telling everyone within earshot what a cad her former husband is. She also hires the most contentious lawyer she can find, promises to "ruin the creep," and won't even consider dating.

Although Julia certainly would have preferred that her life had not fallen apart, she focuses on what she *can* influence: her attitude, her career, and her relationships. She also refuses to let the situation determine her behavior. She knows—no matter how despicable his behavior— her husband can not *make* her react in any way. She has free will. She can decide whether she really wants to call him names, adopt a victim posture, and wallow in self-pity, or negotiate a fair settlement, get a better job, and forge new relationships. She doesn't react; she decides. Sarah, on the other hand, reacts to the rejection in ways that she says she can't help. "After all," she says, "he *makes* me vindictive." She has surrendered control over her own emotions to a husband who has cheated on her. By doing so, she empowers him and weakens her own position.

In fact, every time you feel bad because someone rejects you, or lose confidence in an idea because someone criticizes it, or avoid expressing yourself because someone might not like what you have to say, you are putting your need for approval ahead of your other needs. You are demonstrating that you only feel worthwhile if others indicate that you are; you only have confidence in your ideas if others support them, and you only say what you think if it will make others see you in a favorable light. Basically, you are operating under the belief that since your happiness is determined by others—and you certainly can't *control* how others think or behave—you have little influence over your own happiness. This victim's mindset puts you at the whim of people all around you. Operating under such a paradigm, you will not feel the self-confidence necessary for inner peace, nor are you likely to get what you want in life.

Have you ever heard someone say, "Oh, she *made* me lose my temper" or "I *had* to give in because she was so insistent" or "They *always* push my buttons"? Perhaps you have even said similar things yourself...when you were feeling manipulated and overwhelmed by your emotions. But consider this: when you blame other people for *your* response to *their* behavior, you are basically saying that others—not you—are in control. You are giving away power every time you indicate that you can't help doing something. Certainly, you can not control how others behave, but—and this is a big but—you *can* control how you respond. When a store clerk treats you badly, you may *react* by feeling annoyed, but you do not have to *act* rudely yourself. When someone is late for a business appointment, you might *feel* slighted, but you do not have to *behave* irresponsibly by being late yourself next time. Instead, you can put yourself in the driver's seat by deliberately choosing a response that will still feel right a few hours later. When you control your impulses by responding deliberately instead of reacting in a knee-jerk fashion, you are taking responsibility for your actions.

People with self-mastery take responsibility for their choices; they do not blame others for their decisions or their problems. Upon receiving an invitation that doesn't fit within plans, a self-master might simply say, "Thank you, but I'm visiting my sister on Saturday." Someone less self-responsible might assume a victim's stance, saying, "Oh, I'd love to, but I *have* to visit my sister on Saturday." When late for an appointment, a self-confident person would accept responsibility, saying something like, "My apologies; I did not plan enough travel time." Someone less confident might say, "I'm sorry I'm late...Bob just wouldn't let me off the phone." When asked to help out on a prescheduled afternoon, a self-master might say, "Oh, I'm sorry; I've got a project due this afternoon." Someone less independent might say, "I would, but my boss will fire me if I don't finish this report." Mastery is about taking charge of your own emotions and controlling knee-jerk reactions that you might later regret. It is about taking responsibility for all of your actions and deliberately deciding how to respond to the behavior of others.

To feel confident and capable of influencing your life, try to become more internally motivated, seeking self-validation instead of approval from others. Remind yourself that no matter what anyone else says or does, you are a worthwhile person. No matter what obstacles are put in your path, you will be able to cope. No matter how despicably anyone behaves, you can choose an appropriate response...a response that fits with the kind of person you want to be and the goals you are trying to achieve. You can determine what you want and go after it, rather than *wishing* others would change their behavior. Regardless of the difficulties you face, your choice is always the same: take responsibility for making the situation better or live with the consequences.

Several years ago, at a time when I was feeling overworked and under-appreciated, a good friend reminded me that although I always gave a good deal to others, I didn't ask for much myself. "Who takes care of you?" she asked. At the time, I just wept. I thought that "no one" was the only honest answer. Since then I have come to realize that while we may have many supportive and loving people in our lives, the only healthy answer to that question is "I do." If you don't believe that your health is important, no one else can help. If you don't ask for what you want, your best supporters won't know what to give. If you don't manage your own time, there will be no time for you.

MANAGE TIME INTENTIONALLY

Although we are all given the same 24 hours every day, some people seem to manage a rich life full of achievement, adventure, love, and pleasure, while others never "have the time." When I was young, I never quite understood what my mother meant when she would say, "If you want something done, ask a busy person." Back then, it made no sense. Years later, it makes perfect sense. The most accomplished people I know are busy in many areas of life. I've worked with CEOs who run companies, but also climb mountains, spend time with their families, stay physically fit, and serve their communities on nonprofit boards. Many artists earn their living through their craft, while also studying the work of masters, developing innovative techniques, mentoring young artists, and volunteering for important causes like A.I.D.S. or abolition of landmines. Several teachers I've met devote incredible hours to preparing and conducting classes and still manage to assume leadership roles in their churches, entertain friends, read voraciously, attend the theater, take graduate courses, and serve as a rescue net for family members as needed.

How do they do it? More importantly, how can *you* do it? Or, if you are one of those people, how can you do it more effortlessly? These are the questions for which there are no "right" answers. Each of us is unique in terms of purpose, paradigms, and energy. However, a few elements of effective time management—priorities, planning, and discipline—seem to be used consistently by successful people of many different temperaments.

Focus on priorities. Most successful people do not see any virtue in being overworked, overscheduled, or overwrought. In fact, my experience has been that they have a clear picture of their priorities and aim for a balanced life. They seem to pride themselves on reaching their goals and having time for family, fun, and life-expanding adventures. While most agree that it isn't easy to find balance between one's personal and professional lives, many do it.

In a recent article in *Fast Company* magazine several managers, vice presidents, and directors were asked to address the balance issue. One director of new business development spoke of how she knew it was time to get balance when her daughter told her "It'll be all right." She also said that she regains focus by taking three important steps: doing something for herself every day, constantly finding ways to simplify her life, and doing something "recreational" when she feels her work energy waning. A director at a computer company in Texas said that it's easy to make balance a priority when you realize that it actually improves your effectiveness and helps your career. He schedules routine breaks in the workday for reflecting silently or talking with someone important to him. He also said that he is beginning to manage his personal life as if it were a business.

If you work around the clock on a regular basis and want to change, you might reflect on possible causes behind your work-until-I-drop mentality. Is it possible that you do not have the self-esteem to believe that you deserve a life of ease or that you are not too skilled at time management? Is it possible that you are escaping from something? Perhaps you are chasing after the wrong goals (somebody else's instead of your own) or getting trapped in a work culture that encourages an unhealthy work style.

To focus on how you can gain more balance in your life ask yourself a few questions. First, *"How much time do you want to devote to your job each week, excluding occasional glitches or emergencies?"* Consider how much time you need to accomplish your goals and at what point your effectiveness actually decreases, making working any longer counterproductive.

Secondly, *"What is it that you want to make time for in your life...your partner, children, exercise, silence, a walk in the park?"* If you make what you want to include a priority, putting it on your to-do list as you would any work task, it's more likely you will actually do it. All too often we put personal renewal breaks on a "when-I-have-time" list which literally gets pushed to the rear of our days.

Third, *"What reward are you receiving for letting work usurp all of your waking hours?"* Is it possible that you receive sympathy or someone's approval? Might you be escaping from something? Often an overly hectic pace is a way of avoiding an issue we don't want to face.

Create a powerful plan. Taking responsibility for your own success means more than dreaming and setting quarterly goals. You've got to translate your plan into a list of actions or subtasks related to each of your broad goals. Then you need to decide how long each action will take, what information or resources you will need to accomplish each, and how you will know when you have succeeded. Your plan for happiness will serve as your compass. You will know exactly where you're going at all times. You will notice clarity of purpose, an increased sense of urgency, renewed energy, and enhanced confidence as you meet the milestones you have identified on the road to your destination.

Busy people with balanced lives usually plan ahead. They know how much time something will take to accomplish, when it needs to be complete, and where it can be scheduled into the week. They wake up in the morning knowing what they need to do first. They know before they make a telephone call, what points they want to make and what outcomes they hope to see. They know on Friday what their next week's goals are, and what they'll have to do to accomplish them. They can be interrupted or take a spontaneous break and get right back on target because what they intend to achieve is always in the forefront of their minds; their direction is crystal clear. They know their goals and are intent on achieving them. They recognize which actions will move them forward, which will maintain status quo, and which will actually send them back a milestone or two. Such planning allows "mini-vacations" (such as twenty minutes to reflect in silence and recenter yourself) by providing assurance that work is under control.

Keeping a sharp focus means surrounding yourself with reminders of what it is that you want in your life. Some success coaches suggest writing your primary goals (be a better father, 25% increase in income, a score of 90 at golf, vacation in Hawaii) on a 3"x 5" card to carry in your wallet and read several times a day. Others suggest creating a wall collage of magazine photos for your workspace...one picture representing each of your goals. Frame each picture in gold as the goal is achieved. Another strategy to help you stay focused is to create a picture of you in your target. You might paste your photo on a cover of *People* magazine, write the title of your new book in the number one spot on a copy of *The New York Times* bestseller list, or create a "virtual" bank statement to show your first one million-dollar deposit.

Many professional sports coaches, management consultants, and inspirational leaders have said that visualizing a positive outcome as if it were already a reality increases the probability of success. Focus on what you want...often and in detail. Dream in Technicolor.

Discipline yourself. Even armed with a clear focus and a great plan, you can still veer off course if you are not disciplined. There will be many opportunities for you to interrupt your day with unimportant things. You'll have to decide when these self-interruptions are likely to be fruitful (e.g., taking a walk to clear your head, stopping for water to reverse fatigue, brainstorming with someone) and when they are merely avoidance techniques such as getting coffee, sorting mail, or returning low-priority calls.

You also have to be assertive about limiting interruptions from others. Obviously, there are some interruptions that are important and welcomed (an inquiry for your services, a thank-you visit from a colleague, a request for input from your boss, a call from your teenager that she was accepted into your alma mater). The first trick is in quickly distinguishing urgent/important interruptions from non-urgent or unimportant interruptions such as coworker chitchat, vendor solicitations, or calls for information that has already been sent. The second trick is to maintain a relationship while assertively blocking the interruption. You'll have to be firm, polite, brief, and clear.

Of course, the best protection against interruptions is prevention. You can close your door, move out of the range of sight, practice a hold-all-calls hour, communicate specific "open door" times, let others know under what circumstances you'd like to be interrupted, or post a "genius at work" sign on your door. Whether the interruptions in your day are self-induced or prompted by others, make an effort to reduce them if you want to achieve more in your life.

To take responsibility for a fulfilling life is to choose how you use each day of your life. Check any self-sabotaging habits, let go of old anger and resentment, become response-able, take care of yourself, and manage your time intentionally. ⋍

CHAPTER *3*

create "tenant" rules
        for thoughts
in your mind

if they don't behave,
        evict 'em

DECORATE THE ROOMS
OF YOUR MIND AS YOU WOULD
A FAVORITE RETREAT...
WITH THINGS THAT
CALM YOUR SPIRIT AND
FIRE YOUR IMAGINATION.

S. W. Z.

CHAPTER *3*

create "tenant" rules
for thoughts in your mind

*b*eliefs and behaviors are
inextricably linked. It has been said by many that our
thoughts create our reality. If the inner messages we hear
are of growth, love, and joy...that will be our experience.
If, on the other hand, we give "air time" to thoughts of
limitations, fear, and failure...that is what we will experience. Henry Ford once said, "If you believe you can or you
believe you can't...you're right." To be all that you aspire
to be, you will need to decorate the rooms of your mind as
you would a favorite retreat...with things that calm your
spirit and fire your imagination.

In my personal growth workshops, I often open
with a poll of the participants by asking three questions to
relax and focus the group. First, I ask: "How many of you
talk to yourself?" This usually prompts laughter and a sea
of nodding heads. Then I ask, "What is it that you most
often say?" This question generates painful grimaces of

recognition. Finally I ask, "Are your internal dialogues uplifting?" Expressions of insight light up the room. Unless asked to focus on our mind conversations, we typically play the same mental "tapes" day in and day out, without considering either the quality of the messages or the impact they have on our attitudes.

To better understand the mind/body connection, consider the last time you thought, "I'm getting sick and tired of this job (the weather, a relationship, or life in general)." Chances are that soon after you started running that mindtape, you actually got sick. Or, try to remember what happened to your energy the last time you answered, "Fabulous" when someone asked how you were. You probably got a jolt of energy that quickened your pace and automatically made you smile.

Perhaps an experiment will demonstrate the principle. First, lower your head, slouch in your chair, and say out loud, "I feel fit and fabulous!" It doesn't work, does it? Now, jump to your feet, thrust your arms overhead, make fists like Rocky Balboa, and shout, "I feel depressed." That doesn't work either because your mind and body are not in sync. The mixed signals have created dissonance within your system. If you continued to think, "I'm depressed," but behaved like a victor, your system would self-adjust. Either your mood would elevate or your grand gesture would fizzle. That's why if you're feeling angry and someone makes you smile, you suddenly feel less angry.

You cannot hold onto a negative emotion while you are physically behaving in a positive fashion. Your thoughts and body are wired together. Every time you think, "I'm tired," you transmit a powerful signal throughout your body to "behave tired." Expect your body to respond with heavy eyelids, poor posture, reduced energy. On the other hand, when you think or say, "I feel great," you send a signal to your control center to "resume peak performance mode." Expect your adrenaline to pump, your endorphins to rise, and your energy to climb. Each day give yourself a lift by saying often, "I love my life."

The mind/body connection has been well documented by many medical experts and authors. If you'd like to explore this area further, consider reading one of the many best-selling books on the topic such as: *Ageless Body, Timeless Mind* by Deepak Chopra, M.D., *Spontaneous Healing* by Andrew Weil, M.D., and *Timeless Healing* by Herbert Benson, M.D. It is safe to assume that positive thought, prayer, and meditation have a positive impact on our health and well-being.

Seven simple techniques that have helped many people to maintain a positive mindset are described in this chapter. You can enhance your confidence and competency by using affirmations, evictions, visualizations, reframing, solution sleuthing, balcony viewing, and esteem feeding. See if any of them appeal to you as tools you might use to tap your reservoir of positive energy.

PRACTICE THE ART OF AFFIRMATIONS

Although we all experience ongoing "mind chatter" (at about 200 words per minute), you can consciously choose the *kind* of chatter that occupies your mind. One way to do this is to develop and use a list of personal affirmations. An affirmation is positive self-talk. You might think of an affirmation as a wish that you state as if it had already come true. For instance, if you *wish* you were a better father, a more thoughtful lover, and a successful investor, an appropriate affirmation could be "I *am* a terrific father, a sensitive lover, and a wise investor." To be effective, affirmations should be phrased in the present tense (*"I am,"* not *"I will be"*) and in the positive (*"I am calm"* vs. *"I'm not nervous"*). Consider what you would like to be, feel or have. Then write an affirmation for each. You might create daily affirmations that you recite at the beginning and end of each day or situationally-specific affirmations for occasions such as delivering an important speech (*"I am calm, prepared, and entertaining"*). Consider using professional achievement affirmations (*"I am exceeding my goals"*) and personal achievement affirmations (*"I am fit and energetic"*). Repeat your statement confidently, as if it is true...soon it will be. Here are some sample affirmations that you might consider. Modify them, combine them, or write your own.

"I am lovable and capable."
"I am enough, just the way I am."
"I am fit and beautiful."
"I have everything I need to be happy."
"I ask for what I want."
"I am nonjudgmental with myself and others."
"I am neither above nor below anyone else."
"I make a difference every day."
"I bond with others easily."
"I am humble, patient, and compassionate."
"I give something away every day."
"I am fulfilling my purpose and using my unique gifts."
"I love my life."

It is important to determine what is most important to you and write related affirmations so that you can focus your mental energy on your priorities many times throughout a day. Suppose the three most important things to you just now are to make a difference, be physically fit, and experience unbridled love. Your daily affirmation might be similar to one of these.

"I feel great; I make a difference;
great love surrounds me."
"My body is fit; I am loved;
and I love making the world a better place."
"I am so happy to be healthy, loved,
and of service to others."

Consider posting your affirmations on your mirror, in your daily planner, on a telephone or computer screen, or anywhere else you will see them several times a day. I make a practice of saying my affirmations every morning before I get out of bed and every night before I fall off to sleep. I also post daily affirmations next to my office telephone, in my daily planner, or on my computer. Some people tell me they recite their daily affirmations as often as 20 to 30 times in a day. Some write the affirmations on a small card to carry in their wallet. Use whatever method will remind you several times each day of the kind of person you are becoming and the kind of life you are in the process of creating. Let these affirmations keep your mental focus forward on your progress and potential. To see it, repeat it...in your thoughts, images, words, and daily deeds. Think great, do great, and remind yourself regularly that you *are* great!

BECOME A MASTER AT EVICTIONS

The more you fill your mind with positive self-talk, the less room there will be for negative talk. However, that does not mean that a negative thought won't slip in from time to time. Look over the list below to see if—before now—any of these disabling thoughts have been tenants in your mind. Perhaps you'll think of a few others that are no longer welcome.

"I always mess up."

"No one really loves me."

"I can't count on anyone."

"I'll never be able to..."

"I don't want to, but I should..."

"This must be perfect."

"I'm so dumb."

"Bad things always happen to me."

"I'm going to get sick or have an accident."

"I just can't cope anymore."

"I've got to make them happy."

"My life stinks."

"It's not right to say how I really feel."

Old habits die hard, so if a disabling message shows up, get in the habit of booting it out. That's right. As soon as you hear a negative thought, hit the pause button, and say out loud, "Evict that thought. That was before. *This* is my belief now: I am _____." Erase the thought from your mind's computer and replace it with an empowering thought. Make a commitment to evict any "rowdy regulars" the next time they show up.

CREATE GREAT VISUALIZATIONS

What do sports coaches, success gurus, and inspirational writers all have in common? They all believe in the power of imagining your success before you actually create it. All believe that if in a relaxed state you can see yourself—in great detail and living color—successfully performing a feat *before* you actually perform it, you will etch a pattern of success into your brain that will guide you to success in the physical realm. This practice is so commonly endorsed that you won't have to look very far to find star athletes mentally rehearsing a competition before they ever enter an arena. You'll find top salespeople view (in their mind's eye) a vivid documentary of their sales pitch before they ever show up at a prospect's door. The most dynamic keynote speakers deliver their words to thundering applause many times over (on the big screen in their mind) before they actually step up to a podium.

This important habit of success allows you to perform every challenge twice: first with your imagination and then with your feet. Wayne Dyer wrote a wildly successful book on the importance of visualization. *You'll See It When You Believe It* describes how to succeed with the practice of visualization by attending to important elements such as being in a relaxed state, including specific detail, and focusing on a positive outcome. The next time you are faced with a challenge, find a quiet place and take a few deep breaths. Begin by seeing yourself—dressed appropriately—moving toward your performance spot. Note details such as what you are carrying, what the temperature is like, and who else is there. Feel how excited you are for the opportunity and how confident you are that you will succeed. See all the details as you progress from one successful phase to another, until finally you complete your objective and leave the site feeling fulfilled.

You might think of visualization as a series of affirmations in pictures. If you acquire the habit of using both, you will soon see many positive changes in your life. Take a tip from top performers...for success in your field, first see the success in your mind.

LEARN TO REFRAME SITUATIONS

The difference between optimism and pessimism is often described as seeing the glass half-full or seeing the glass half-empty. Reframing is a technique that enables you to see the glass "half-full" more often. Whenever you are faced with a setback or disappointment, look beyond the obvious negative to see if there is any positive consequence, no matter how small. For instance, if you get stuck in traffic—clearly an annoyance to most of us—consider if any good could come of that. You might find that it is the only time all day that you will have to reflect in silence, or you might find that you hear a radio interview that you would not have heard otherwise. Perhaps the 20 minutes is exactly what you need to mentally prepare for the meeting that you are racing to. Instead of framing the traffic jam in cheap red plastic, "reframe" it in rich mahogany with a gold leaf trim. Deliberately choose to see whatever good is woven into life's large and small frustrations. Pay attention to the surprise blessings that appear in your life sometimes disguised as mistakes, disappointments, and irritations.

When you were young, you may have owned a kaleidoscope, or perhaps you even collect them today. When you gaze through a kaleidoscope you see a pattern made of many pieces. With the flick of your wrist making just a tiny twist you can create an entirely new image. With exactly the same number, shape, and color of pieces, you create a brand new masterpiece. You transform what you are given into something that delights you. So it is with reframing. Accept what is presented to you and use your personal desires and imaginative mind to transform your situation into something positive.

BECOME A SOLUTION SLEUTH

To maintain positive self-esteem, you must become a master sleuth, someone who can track down creative solutions to almost any dilemma. When you develop a pattern of successfully resolving problems, you trust yourself to handle any new issues that come your way. Such success breeds self-confidence. As you might have guessed, effective problem solving requires an inventive state of mind where a wide range of possibilities can be scanned. To every problem there are many possible and often equally appropriate solutions. Unfortunately, when we are presented with life's problems, we often become fearful that we will fail or get hurt somehow, so we contract, rather than broaden our thinking. We mentally circle the wagons when we are afraid, instead of scouting out a new trail.

Solution sleuthing is a technique to free up your imaginative responses. Instead of stating a problem as a complaint (*I just don't have any time for myself*), turn your next problem into a question (*How can I find one hour each week just for myself?*). To consider the different impact that a complaint or a question has on your creativity, try imagining your initial response to each. If you were presented with the complaint above (*I just don't have any time for myself*) what would be your reaction? Probably, your response would be something like, "I know; life's a rat race. Nobody has any personal time." Likely, you would commiserate with the misery.

Now consider your response to the problem if it were stated as a question (*How can I find one hour each week just for myself?*). Would you feel rather stimulated...as if you were presented with a riddle to solve? Probably, your response would be something like this: "Hmmm. You could try...." It is likely that you would intuitively start scanning your mind for possible solutions.

When you turn complaints into questions, you stimulate your imagination to search for solutions and energize yourself to prepare for action, change, and improvement. Your outlook is on your intent to move to a better place, not on pitying yourself for being stuck in your present murky spot. To turn your life around at any time, and move quickly from problems to solutions, get in the habit of rephrasing all "complaints" as questions. This simple shift will have a strong impact on the level of satisfaction in your life and on your confidence in yourself to fix anything that goes wrong. Try to influence others in your life—at work and at home—to do the same. Ban all complaining, griping, and dead-end wallowing. Insist that—except for very brief cathartic venting—all problems be expressed as questions. Complaints demoralize; questions energize.

GO TO THE BALCONY FOR A BIRD'S EYE VIEW

We sometimes berate ourselves for not accomplishing what we set out to accomplish or for not becoming the kind of person we had hoped to become. When we do so, it is typically because we are viewing our lives from a very narrow perspective. At that moment we are focusing only on what we have not accomplished. We are seeing only part of the picture.

To improve your perspective, climb—in your mind's eye—to a balcony that overlooks a greater span of your life. From that vantage point, you can get a much clearer view. Look behind you to see where you were a year or two ago. Notice along the trail that brought you to your present space the many markers of success, integrity, and kindness. Observe every fork in the road where you chose the right path: giving rather than withholding, loving instead of judging, and learning instead of stagnating. Within this broadened landscape, you will notice your wise choices as well as your mistakes. Contemplate how every step, on and off the right path, falls into place. What was the purpose of each in your progress journey?

While you are way up in the balcony, you might take the opportunity to toss a few regrets to the wind. Instead of beating yourself up about what you *should* have accomplished in the past, simply move any important unattained goals into your field of potential straight ahead. Whenever you find yourself feeling impatient at what you haven't done, try bringing yourself back to center by repeating this mental phrase: *"No regrets, just firm intentions."*

To keep your accomplishments in the foreground of your mind, you might try keeping a "Success Journal." In a small notebook or steno pad, date and list achievements that make you proud of yourself. Your list might include accomplishments as large as completing a college degree program, closing a deal at work, or losing ten pounds. It might include interpersonal successes such as not yelling at your teenager, remembering to write a thank-you note, or negotiating a win/win solution with a coworker. You can paste in congratulatory or thank-you notes from friends and kudos from your boss. Note any goals set and accomplished on time. Read through it at least once a week, and more often when you seem to be in a slump. It will help you to remember your potential.

Still another way to maintain perspective is to reframe all mistakes as "opportunities to learn." Some weeks it might feel as though you're going for an advanced degree, but hang in there anyway. If you lose your temper with a coworker, apologize and then reflect quietly about what you learned from the incident. Perhaps you learned that you shouldn't try to deal with differences when your blood sugar is low. Or maybe you learned that you can be more objective if you mentally rehearse what you are going to say before you actually say it. You might have learned that a particular issue is more important to you than you realized. When you don't succeed at something, you are being presented with an opportunity to learn something important about yourself. If you don't pay attention, you will most likely be presented with a similar opportunity again...and again...until you learn the lesson.

FEED YOUR ESTEEM

Walt Disney, arguably one of the most creative minds of our time, believed that self-esteem was the most important factor in realizing dreams. He wrote, "Somehow I can't believe that there are any heights that can't be scaled by a man who knows the secrets of making dreams come true. This special secret, it seems to me, can be summarized in four C's. They are curiosity, confidence, courage, and constancy...and the greatest of all is confidence. When you believe in a thing, believe in it all the way, implicitly and unquestionably."

It takes regular doses of fertilizer to grow a garden of sturdy positive thoughts. Have you ever noticed how you can be "up" one week and so down on yourself the next? Here are a few ideas to keep you "up" more steadily.

• Write down four to five of your most outstanding personal strengths and post the list where you can be reminded (every time you pass by) of the special gifts that you have been given. Your list might include such things as patience, warmth, insight, humor, generosity, empathy, intelligence, compassion, loyalty, spirituality, perseverance, creativity, etc. If you prefer, write your unique qualities in the front of a journal...just remember to review the list every now and then. You can also ask close friends and family what they consider your most positive personal qualities.

• Try keeping an S.T.A.R. (simple thanks and recognition) folder with notes and reminders of where you have excelled and where you have made a difference. When I review my own folder every now and then, I am reminded of how tiny acts of kindness which take so little effort can mean so much to others.

• On the last day of every month (yes, 12 times a year!) list all of your accomplishments. They can be as small as "Ate bran muffins every week" and "Cleaned my closet" or as large as "Closed the deal in Australia" and "Tobacco-free for 30 days." Just list everything you did in the last month that you consider a success. You can post the list until you generate a new one and then file past lists in your S.T.A.R. folder.

• Reflect in silence every day through prayer, meditation, or communing with nature. Close your door and sit comfortably for five minutes, particularly halfway through your day. Open a window if you can, or take a five-minute walk outside; breathe in the fresh air. Sit by running water, listen to the rain, or just concentrate on the beating of your heart. Move your chair to a window and bask for a moment or two in the warmth of the sun. Take a five-minute respite in the middle of your day to reflect, pose a question, recite a prayer, or just sit and find some inner peace. ⌒

As I lift my face to the Sun's warm rays
I find myself in prayer:
"Soothe my soul so it will heal;
Light the way so I might learn.
Warm my heart so I'll know love;
Empower me to serve."

S. W. Z.

CHAPTER *4*

take your passions for a walk every day

enjoy, embrace,
and celebrate

WATCH THE BALLET OF
LIGHTNING BUGS ON A HOT,
HUMID NIGHT OR BARN SWALLOWS
IN FLIGHT AT DUSK...
WHAT BETTER GIFTS ARE
THERE THAN THESE?

S. W. Z.

CHAPTER *4*

take your passions for a walk every day

W hen we are striving to support ourselves, get ahead, and "make it," the trappings of success—a good income, professional accomplishments, a zillion adult toys—all are indicators that we have "arrived." But, as we come face to face with our own mortality, "arriving" begins to feel more like "over the hill." With time flying by at an ever-increasing speed, we become acutely aware of how much time we have spent in "acquiring" and how little time we have spent in savoring what we already have. It often takes an illness or loss to remind us that life's real treasures are often found in our own back yard and we should treasure what we have.

Midlifers who have found inner peace and decided to fully embrace life in the second half often share their vitality and zest for life with others. Their sensuality draws you near, their centered nature inspires you to follow, and their spontaneous joy warms you at your core.

They radiate an energy that perpetuates optimism and focuses on expansion. In the reflection of such people we often see the best parts of ourselves.

When I am in the presence of these exuberant souls I am reminded of a principle from my early days of dance training. When I was in college I performed with a travelling dance company. One of the very first techniques that the women in the company were taught was how to allow yourself to be lifted with ease. Regardless of the strength of the male dancer or relative weight of the female dancer, the key to a well-executed lift is in the "liftee." A dancer can either prepare to fly by contracting her muscles and using the support offered, becoming light as a feather, or she can drop her weight and become a ton of bricks, making the lift almost impossible. In much the same way, it seems to me, passionate people allow themselves to be lifted. They don't hold themselves down with the weighty parts of their lives, but instead allow their spirits to be buoyed by the many joys in life. They use the energy of life to reach uncommon heights; in the connection, they soar.

Perhaps you will recognize such passionate people by how revived you feel when you are in their presence. As they inhale the pleasures of life, their passion expands and our own flight is made easier as we catch the updraft from their dynamic ascent.

Bob, a Colorado English teacher who adores writing poetry, says that when he writes, reads, or shares his poetry time stands still. He also loves judging poems for the senior high school's competition, serving on the editorial board of a poetry journal, and mentoring a young poet from his neighborhood. He isn't teaching much poetry at the moment—only one unit each semester—but when he becomes eligible for early retirement in three years, he'd like to teach poetry at the local community college. Once a year he attends a poet's conference/retreat and he just enrolled for a weekend master class led by a cadre of renowned poets.

Carol is passionate about her faith. She reads inspirational books, volunteers at church, and spends time in prayer every day. She gives thanks before meals and regularly praises the wonders of nature as she chirps with delight, "Look, look, isn't that gorgeous? An iris has bloomed." She radiates warmth and is a master of everyday kindness. It is clear that she loves to study, praise, and do the Lord's work every day in many different ways. Where there is pain, she shows compassion; where there is fatigue, she provides energy; where there is interest, she lights the way. She does what she loves...and loves everything she does.

To expand your capacity for aliveness, consider where you can be more fully present in your daily life. Enjoy all that is within your reach, embrace your potential for much more, and celebrate with gratitude.

ENJOY ALL THAT IS WITHIN REACH

How much time do you spend enjoying what absolutely delights you? Passions soothe your soul and renew your spirit, so why deny yourself? Life is beautiful and meant to be fully enjoyed. Indulge yourself with your favorite treats often...and without guilt.

What delights your senses? Know what foods, activities, and pleasures delight your senses. Keep a list of the tastes that make your mouth water, the scents that you always wish would linger, and the little pleasures that make you feel like a member of a royal family. Organize your list by seasons or locales, if you wish, but keep it near to remind you of your desires and prompt you to enjoy them more often. A body massage, a lunch in the park, a special blend of coffee, a decadent dessert, classical music, a yoga session, jazz with a friend, an hour in your favorite art gallery, a walk along the beach...what tickles you? Don't wait for special occasions or for when you have more time or money. Deliberately delight your senses today.

So often we don't even enjoy what has been beautifully presented to us by Mother Nature. We rush in from the rain instead of indulging in the stimulating sensations that wash over us in a storm. We sleep past sunrises and work past sunsets, yet these are pleasures that don't cost a dime. We crush a ladybug without giving a second glance toward its crimson enamel wings. We shut out the laughter of children on the street and the wakeup call of cardinals at dawn. Yet as children we were keenly aware of it all. At midlife we feel more alive if we remember the habit of seeing the world through a child's eyes. For enhanced vitality, adopt an attitude of wonder and fall in love with life all over again.

Smell the scent of honeysuckle in the perfumed air that follows a spring rain. Listen for the gentle song of wrens and the sound of escalating winds. Watch the ballet of lightning bugs on a hot humid night or barn swallows in flight at dusk. Enjoy the taste of wild berries whether gathered fresh or bought at a local market. A radiant sunrise, a sultry sunset, hemlock branches laden with snow...what better gifts are there than these? See the beauty in all that's near and bring it closer to you. Stop and pick a roadside cluster of Queen Anne's Lace, sit where the winter sun streams through a window, or watch a chickadee build a nest for its young out of twigs and lime-green moss. Plant an orange seed in a little paper cup and watch it grow to a glossy green. Take pleasure in the simple riches that surround us all.

What touches you? What is it that touches you so deeply that you could almost weep? Perhaps it is listening to Vivaldi's *Four Seasons* or reading a verse by your favorite poet. Or maybe it is hearing an inspirational speaker, watching a ballet, or being courtside at an NBA playoff. Among such delights in my life I include watching great dancers perform and listening to opera sung by Pavarotti, Lesley Garrett, or my friend Anne, who has an angel's voice. There is a magical alignment of sensibilities when we are fortunate enough to glimpse great gifts. Consider what you were enjoying the last time you felt your heart leap, and commit to enjoying that pleasure more frequently.

Sometimes it is not awe, but sheer joy that awakens the heart. Perhaps it is a cocker spaniel wagging its whole body to greet you, a naked two-year-old romping on the beach, or the silly dance of two squirrels circling the trunk of a tree in playful pursuit of each other's tail. What tickles you so that you simply cannot repress a smile?

Recently I stopped to talk with a neighbor while I was out walking my dog. She told me that her little poodle had passed away and though she missed her companion, she didn't feel she should get another dog since her life was rather full taking care of a husband in poor health. I was feeling great sadness for her loss when suddenly her whole countenance shifted and a big smile came across her face. "But," she said, "I do have a pet squirrel. His name is Topsy and he comes to be fed twice a day. I allow him onto the breezeway, but he knows he cannot come into the house. Sometimes he brings his whole family, but they wait outside. I throw them nuts." The joy of a "pet" is within everyone's reach.

What brings you inner peace? Some enjoyment fills the senses and some wraps around our hearts, and then there is the kind of enjoyment that brings a serene awareness from within. Perhaps for you that enjoyment comes in the form of basking in the sun or reflecting in church while listening to a lovely choir. Maybe it's walking in the woods or gazing up through a canopy of leaves from your hammock. I find peace by meditating near water, sitting in silence by a fire, or tending to my 12-year-old perennial garden. When my hands are in the soil gently prodding potential from plants, I find unusual peace...it's a kind of reverie for me. You can't help but feel serene in this lovely space where the garden and its riverbed rock wall were beautifully designed to harmonize with nature.

My father-in-law, Harry, also found peace in his garden. When he bought his first house at age 67, I remember how relatives and friends all tried to convince him that it was a mistake. They said he should be considering a retirement village, not a house with a yard to keep. But Harry wanted a small patch of land for his tomatoes, so he bought that house and lived to harvest many crops of tomatoes.

The first year in his new house, Harry decided to plant a few maple saplings—one in the back yard so he would have a shady place to read the Sunday paper on summer afternoons. My husband and I were full of youth's arrogance back then, and I remember how we scoffed at that scrawny tree. When Dad was out of earshot we'd chuckle at how foolishly optimistic he was to think that he would live long enough to witness a canopy of leaves from that puny little maple. Well, you won't be surprised to learn that Dad did live to sit in the shade of that little tree. The first summer that the maple provided enough shade for lazing was Dad's last summer. Home from the hospital, riddled with cancer, he found a few last blissful moments reading his paper in the cool comfort of the tree that only he ever envisioned as a "shade tree."

Who brings out the zest in you? To rev up your passion and tap more of your life potential consider connecting more often with those who make you feel alive, spontaneous, and optimistic. Surround yourself with wisdom, intuition, wit, humor, and childlike innocence. Know who it is that makes you feel loved and joyful. Consider who makes you laugh easily and who, in easing nuggets of self-awareness from you, encourages you to be honest with yourself. Strengthen connections with those who generously exchange learnings, explore ideas with you, and listen nonjudgmentally when you share your thoughts. Celebrate life with those who know you, warts and all...those with whom you have a loving history...so you can enjoy without pretense and dance to the music playing in your soul.

One of my friends has the most endearing habit of greeting my telephone calls with, "Oh, it's so good to hear your voice." She is a busy working mom who is also an elected official and a community volunteer, but she is never too busy to make me feel cherished. Such generosity of love always inspires me to pass along love to the next person I meet.

Another friend is a surefire guarantee for hearty laughter. She doesn't tell jokes or stories; she just sees the humor in life's little episodes. She laughs easily, and her laughter is infectious. She reminds all who come in contact with her to lighten up and honor the innocent exuberance of the child we all carry inside. Norman Cousins, in his now famous book on the power of laughter (*Anatomy of an Illness*), convinced us of the power of laughter to heal and promote well-being. The endorphins that are released boost our immune system as well as our spirit. Laugh often, and laugh heartily.

Still another friend can be counted on to energize. He has great enthusiasm for food, wine, opera, laughter...and life in general. It's impossible not to get a "boost" when you're in his presence.

Other friends are comforting, accessible, and supportive. Some stretch my mind; others warm my heart. Some honor me with their secret fears, plans, or challenges. All are treasures that add immensely to my life. Consider who brings out the best in you...and beat a path to their door more often.

EMBRACE YOUR POTENTIAL FOR MUCH MORE

Passion in life stems from a forward focus. If we are not growing, learning, and evolving, we will begin to wither inside. Our energy will wane and our vitality will weaken. For enhanced passion at midlife, try moving toward new horizons as they appear. Do not wait for them to come to you.

If you have thoughts of playing the guitar, volunteering at a local museum, or learning conversational French, that is what to expand in your life. Even if you can only listen to guitar music on your way to work, visit a museum once a month, or play French tapes once a week...do it. Move toward anything that holds the potential to enliven your life.

What passions do you long to indulge? Perhaps you've always wanted to study painting, learn to tap dance or become a weekend disc jockey. Maybe you've been meaning to audition for a local choral or theater group. How about that children's story that you started a year ago? We often say that there is not enough time, but we all have the same 24 hours in a day. Continue your journey to a more satisfying life by making time for your passions. Choose to spend your time in ways that add zest to your life. Diminish time habits that are not yielding the renewed energy that you need to make the second half of your life the *best* half.

Consider getting up one hour earlier each day. That would give you 365 extra hours, 15 extra days, or over 45 extra eight-hour blocks of time per year to do whatever it is you'd really like to do. Think of all that you could do with more than three eight-hour blocks of time per month. That's the equivalent of three work days "off" each month to embrace what you love or experience adventures that would expand your world. You might find time for meditating, exercising, reading, writing, painting, or visiting with friends...all by getting up only one hour earlier each day.

Or you might consider re-allocating some discretionary time to something that you'd find more life expanding. For instance, instead of reading a novel before bed each night, one night a week you could read inspirational material; instead of renting a sad movie for Friday night, you could rent a performance of the *Three Tenors in Rome*. Rather than go to the same pizza place around the corner, you could cook up a "custom" pizza with a friend. Make room for something you've not done before by doing less of something that neither expands your mind nor tickles your soul.

In a hurried world, joy is often found hiding in the details. Think of the difference between drinking eight ounces of water from a plastic bottle on your way out the door and sipping water from a crystal goblet with a lemon slice floating on top. People with passion pay attention, and whether it is in the presentation of food, the wrapping on a gift, or the details of a story they are relaying, they seem to release the full potential for delight.

I love fresh flowers and usually have them in my home year-round, but only recently started placing them in my dressing area. Now, the first thing I see in the morning and the last thing I see at night are details of nature's wonder. I don't know why it took so long to add such a small detail that gives me such a delicious lift every morning.

A few years ago I made another minor change that resulted in a major shift. I moved my office from a windowless business complex into my home. Now I write with the sun streaming in two windows and my cocker spaniel, Sasha, comfortably curled up nearby...or reminding me that it's time to take a walk. My garden is right outside for mind-clearing breaks and I can comfortably work in the early morning hours or well into the night. My commute is perfect and I can even wear slippers if I like. The details make the difference.

It is clear that we don't have to become victims of routine, allowing vitality to seep out of our lives. We can add spark, enthusiasm, and passion to our lives by innovating in any number of ways. Take the scenic route to work, find an exotic takeout restaurant to challenge your senses, or scout out a new spot to watch the sun set. Design a different pamper-yourself afternoon, read a whole new genre of books, learn about a foreign culture, or listen to a category of music you've never really explored before. Ask someone you'd like to meet to lunch, join a new chat room on the Internet, or call someone you love in the middle of the day. Take up yoga or meditation; join a cycling club or rowing crew. Run a marathon, build a birdhouse, or paint your front door red. A sense of aliveness is reinforced every time you move out of your comfort zone to change even one element of your life.

CELEBRATE WITH GRATITUDE

Besides enjoying what surrounds you and expanding your horizons, another way to feel exquisitely alive is to stop and give thanks for all the blessings in your life. It's nearly impossible to feel deprived when you are showing appreciation for the bounty at your feet. Whether it is a bird's song or a Bach concerto, a bite of dark chocolate or a gourmet feast, the first crocus to bloom or a gorgeous bouquet of lilies...stop, savor, and give thanks. Practice the art of full awareness by revering the sheer beauty around you. Applaud the world's artists (performing and visual) and generously encourage their efforts at making the world a more beautiful place. You can not help but feel truly alive when you are connected to nature, art, and the creative force behind it all.

Celebrate often and with gusto...at work, at home, with friends and lovers. Make birthdays, anniversaries, milestones, and markers memorable occasions. Make signs and life-size cards and string balloons across the room. Dress up in costumes or spruce up the space, but make the moment a special place. Pop the corks, pull out the stops, and recapture the exuberance of a child's surprise. Sing, dance, and play music. Laugh, hug, and tell honoree stories. Make meaningful toasts, capture thoughts on an autograph board, and take photos that will last a lifetime. Kick up your heels and celebrate good health, good friends, and fun...these are life's real treasures.

To fuel the passion in your life enjoy what you have, embrace even more, and celebrate the blessings of nature and friends. Pay attention, step into adventure, and give thanks for all that brightens your life. ⬱

CHAPTER *5*

build bridges
without tolls

create relationships
of caring and trust

MATTERS OF THE HEART
MATTER MOST IN LIFE.

S. W. Z.

CHAPTER *5*

build bridges
without tolls

*A*s children we depend on others for our very survival. Later, we depend on others (parents, bosses, spouses, friends) for affirmation that we are lovable and capable. Eventually—when we have succeeded on our own—we rely less on others for either survival or a sense of self-worth. Ironically, just as we midlifers realize that we really don't need others to affirm ourselves, we discover that we need others to transcend ourselves.

As we face our own mortality and ask the question that resonates in midlife—"Is this all there is?"—we begin to realize that giving of ourselves generates meaning and matters of the heart matter most in life. We seldom hear a dying man say that he wishes he had made more money or a dying woman say that she wishes she had more professional success. More often what we hear are regrets of relationships not fully realized...of life not fully lived. At the end, so many people tell us that they wish they had spent more time with loved ones and appreciated what they had more fully. Unfortunately, it often takes illness, an accident, or a significant loss to open our eyes to the connections we should cherish and to the truth about what is most satisfying in life. But we don't have to wait to learn this lesson in life; we can listen to those who are more experienced and hear the wisdom in our own hearts. It is through relationships of caring, appreciation, and love that we release the best parts of ourselves. As we shift our energy from "doing and accumulating" to "being and giving," self-satisfaction increases and life expands.

BEGIN WITH SELF-LOVE

But to give love generously, you must be able to love yourself. Embrace each day as a new opportunity to acknowledge and affirm yourself. Look in the mirror and acknowledge that you love the person you see. Congratulate yourself every night on all that you handled well that day and forgive yourself for any slips. You might also have to record over a few mental tapes if any disabling messages such as, "I'm stupid," "I'm selfish," or "I'm really ashamed of myself" are popping up. In Chapter Three we discussed the use of daily affirmations. When negative thoughts appear, "evict" them and invite in enabling messages such as "I am self-respecting, generous, and a quick learner." Write down a few enabling thoughts and read them at the same time every day (when you awaken, at noon, and just before you fall off to sleep). You have the power to change all negative messages into new mental statements of worth, love, and competence. If you do so, you will become more open to the great love that surrounds you and you will be able to be more loving yourself. Then you will seek deep connections instead of attention and intimacy instead of activity. You will find love and caring in all the right places...within yourself, with devoted family, sincere friends, and trustworthy associates who share your passions.

GIVE UNCONDITIONALLY

You have heard it said many times before, "what goes around comes around." Love too flows in a circular pattern. The more love we give the more we receive, the more we receive the more love we are able to give and so on. The open flow of love increases our energy, aliveness and passion for life. To succeed in forging strong connections, we must transcend our own ego and move beyond individual fears to a state of unconditional love. This is where we learn the paradox of love: the more you give away, the more you will have. When we reach that special level of sharing, we receive a love that stays with us forever. Bill and Shirley shared such a love.

Bill and Shirley were a devoted couple. Married in their teens, they had been together for over 40 years when Bill was diagnosed with leukemia. Their lives had taken many turns through the years...the birth of four children, the death of their oldest son, Bill's numerous health battles, and now...their final challenge of saying goodbye. Shirley was strong, and she said that she was blessed with loving support from her family and friends. However, when you are separated after so many years of deep connection, the hole in your heart is huge. The silence is deafening. You feel so alone. But once you have loved so deeply, are you ever really alone?

Before Bill passed on, he paid off the mortgage on their modest house, making sure that his bride would not have to worry about a place to live. However, due to some unforeseen circumstances and glitches in the system, Shirley ended up receiving fewer benefits and paying more taxes than either of them had expected. She now needed nearly $5000 to pay off a second mortgage *on the house. It was a shame. Bill had tried so hard to protect her, and now with only weeks to go before her retirement and still grieving with a heavy heart, she was navigating through a sea of bureaucratic forms and survivor benefits. She was overwhelmed by the legal jargon and baffled by the seeming contradictions in the system. She even thought that she might not be able to retire after all, although she wasn't sure she could continue working either. The arthritis in her hands was getting worse with each day at her jewelry assembly job.*

But then...something drew her to a pile of old papers in a desk drawer. Among the papers was an insurance policy...so old that Shirley thought it probably had expired. But, something told her to call the company where Bill had worked. The clerk was pleasant, even sympathetic, but indicated that the policy had probably expired since they didn't do business with that insurance company anymore. "But," she said, "let me make a call just to be sure." Within minutes the clerk called back *and said the policy was still valid, and Shirley could expect a check shortly...a check in the amount of $5000...just what she needed to pay off the mortgage. It was then that she knew she was not alone. In fact, Shirley realized that her Bill was still watching over her, just as he had done for so many years.*

When love is unconditional, the connection is everlasting. All significant relationships—with family, friends, partners, our higher selves, and the universe—are strengthened when we give unconditionally. We bond in depth when we give generously from the heart. If you want to deepen your interactions in life, consider four guidelines that build connections that cannot be broken by time or distance: take the time to understand, take the lead in giving, receive graciously, and work for constancy.

TAKE THE TIME TO UNDERSTAND

Strong connections are built on mutuality...a shared commitment to a respectful and satisfying co-existence. To connect we must get to know the other party. We tie bonds of friendship with threads of understanding. Energy is exchanged as we learn about each other's values, interests, talents, and needs. There is not only an intent to please but also loving attention to *what* would please. Taking the time to understand what is important to others allows us to express love and affection in meaningful ways that will be remembered long after the interaction or physical gifts have faded. Knowing what is personally significant is far more important than the value of gifts or the magnitude of the gesture.

Perhaps at one time or another you have missed the mark in trying to please someone. Maybe you did a favor for a friend that only annoyed them in the end. Or perhaps you put hours into a work project that you thought was a real priority, but found out later that it wasn't very important at all...to either your boss or your client. When we base our giving on the assumption that we know the needs of others, we give a present but withhold highly valued gifts of attention and understanding. At the very core of strong connections is a mutual desire to understand and meet each other's needs. Whether the relationship is intimate, professional, or social, it is important to deepen our understanding of what makes the other person tick. Only then can you recognize and support someone in ways that are meaningful and memorable. To demonstrate love and respect we must pay attention to what others need and honor what they value most.

Ken, a leader in a large service organization, is a bright and dedicated worker. He loves his work and it loves him. The problem was that his job required frequent travel that took him away from his family for long periods of time. His role as a father and husband suffered, and the stress began to take its toll on his health and on the well-being of his family. But it seemed to him that he was between a rock and a hard place: provide for the family materially or provide for the family emotionally. It was clear that he had to make some concessions. He knew he had to reassess what his family needed most.

In a rather drastic career move, he took a cut in pay to take a job with less travel. He also pursued counseling to manage his own stress and enhance his ability to connect with his teenage children. Turning long-ingrained work habits around, he managed to shift his time priorities to honor what was most important to his family: his love, attention, and presence. A good lifestyle, Ken came to understand, is never good if the price you pay for it is a disconnection from those you love. A year or so later, he is seeing great improvement in relationships at home, and no noticeable negatives from the job change...except for a little tightening of the belt. Economizing was a small price to pay for the increased peace and love that now permeates Ken's home.

This principle of understanding the needs of others is important to all relationships including business partnerships. Fisher and Ury, authors of the "Bible" of effective negotiation (*Getting To Yes*), state that you are not ready to negotiate with someone until you can state their needs more accurately and convincingly than they can themselves. Only then should you come to the table. The mistake that most of us make in relationships is to go to the "bargaining table" fully armed with a list of what we want, but with little understanding as to what the other party values most. This puts us in a situation of having no bargaining chips. How can we bargain if we don't know what is meaningful to the other party? Why would people negotiate with us unless they trust that we understand and respect their needs?

Relationships begin with respect and flourish with trust. Before we can demonstrate respect, we must pay attention by asking, listening, and observing. We forge the strongest bonds with people when we show interest in them, letting them know that we care about them, have thought about what they value, and want to help them meet their needs. We may not share preferences or values, but we can respect the right of others to hold them. We can be more successful in relationships if we honor the needs of others, even as we attempt to meet our own needs.

TAKE THE LEAD IN GIVING

Besides giving the gift of understanding, we can strengthen all relationships by taking the lead in giving away what most of us want to receive: acceptance, affection, and guidance.

Our perceptions of the world are influenced in a myriad of ways—by our ethnicity, our education, our failures and successes, our parents and upbringing, our native intelligence and emotional dexterity, our politics and religion, even our gender and age. Our perceptions are, in fact, a by-product of everything we have ever experienced. It stands to reason, then, that seldom will any two of us totally agree on what we consider to be "wise," "foolish," "just," "unfair," "right," "wrong," "good," or "evil." If you want to build bridges, do not stand in judgment of those who believe or behave differently. Every time you label someone else's thought or behavior with terms such as "dumb," "foolish," "selfish," or "weak," you distance yourself from that person. By standing in judgment, you put yourself above the person, implying that you are better somehow and therefore your way is "right."

In fact, all you really know is what you know...your truth. Similarly, others behave according to what they know. That doesn't mean they are "bad" or "unworthy"; they just *are*. To forge deeper connections learn to listen openly, consider suggestions offered, and allow others to make their own choices without fear of being dismissed, degraded, or rejected. Practice acceptance. Frequently, relationship counselors ask their clients, "Which is more important to you...to be right, or to be happy?" If you insist on being right all the time (or *proving* that you are right) your relationships will suffer.

Listen to perceptions, build on what you have in common, and respect each person's right (including yours) to see things from a different light. Even when we have to say difficult things in a relationship, we can learn to become experts in what Buddha called "Right speech." Buddha wrote that we should learn to say things in such a way that others always feel loved, and until we can figure out such a way, we should maintain "noble silence." Speak the truth, but always kindly.

We all need affection as well as acceptance, and fortunately it is such an easy thing to give away. What does it cost to give away an affectionate glance, a warm smile, a friendly handshake, or a great big hug? Yet such well-timed gifts often make the difference in someone's day.

With a quick gesture of caring you can light up a room, fill an empty day, or brighten a gloomy spirit. When you do so (allowing your higher self to take the lead) you will always feel good, taking away much more than you give.

Many years ago my father was in the hospital for what turned out to be his last battle with heart disease. It was difficult watching his bloated body deteriorate along with his former zest for life, but I visited nearly every day and became rather connected with Dad's hospital room-mate who had blinded himself in an attempted suicide. The irony of the situation touched me deeply. My father, a man who loved life lay dying while across the room a man who wanted to die lay facing life, blinded and all alone. Whatever cheer I had to offer I'd share on every visit, but what I took away was by far the greater gift. They both let me know that I made a difference and spoke to me with great affection. Even today it warms my heart when I remember how my father affectionately referred to me as "Pumpkin" and the blind man called me "Sunshine." Terms of endearment often last a lifetime.

With a thoughtful note or a small token of kindness, you can provide a reminder that someone cares. Such touch-stones often become reference points that help us feel the associated love many times over. When we hold such trea-sures in our hands they warm our hearts all over again... as the love behind them washes over us once more.

Sitting prominently on my desk is a small round paperweight of cobalt blue glass embedded with white Venetian millefiori stars. It was given to me by a client and good friend who attached a note that began, "Because you help others reach for the stars...." That lovely little touchstone of appreciation and respect reminds me daily of the kind of person I aspire to be.

My soulmate, Mike, touched me deeply this year by presenting me with a gold brooch...a feather, which is the symbol for the Tickle Your Soul™ series. He made the gift even more special by giving it to me well before completion of the manuscript when—in the depths of final rewrites—I sorely needed a reminder of my soul-tickling intent. I have only to look at that golden feather and my heart swells with love.

A dear friend of mine has literally decorated my home over the years with original and beautifully crafted gifts that she has lovingly made by hand. Quilts, etchings, prints, and decorative pillows all stand as reminders of the deep friendship that we both cherish.

Sometimes the gift that is most needed is guidance. We can take the lead in sharing information, lessons learned, or tips on how to proceed. Of course, this gift is best given when others ask for it, but our openness to sharing will make it easier for others to ask. This gift of ourselves seems especially meaningful in an age when we no longer sit around a fire hearing the wisdom of our ancestors woven through tales of our heritage. We are often disconnected from extended family and even lacking mentors in the workplace. For baby boomers, it is especially significant because we are actually marching into a place no one has ever gone before...into a second adulthood for which there are no pre-established rules. If we can lean on one another, sharing ideas and forming support teams, we may just find our way to the best half of our lives.

RECEIVE GRACIOUSLY

Strong relationships are nurtured by a two-way flow of giving. Receiving graciously is just as important as giving generously. That includes being open to what is offered, asking for what we need, and showing appreciation for all that we receive. Being open to love is not always easy, especially when we have been wounded. It takes a brave heart to risk opening up again. But when you take the risk...the potential for happiness is great, as Doug found out.

Doug, a 54-year-old risk appraiser for an international insurance company, lost the love of his life to pancreatic cancer. She died on the anniversary of Doug's mother's death 12 years before. Although a religious man, Doug's faith seemed to wane as he sank deeper and deeper into grief and depression. There didn't seem to be much reason for going on alone since even God had not answered his prayers. Normally a cheerful soul, he found himself angry, depressed, and near the end of his rope. Friends and family could not comfort him; coworkers did not seem to understand. He was alone with his grief and couldn't seem to find his former focus or motivation.

Then, one day he decided to go to church services, after which he reached out to another member of the congregation to congratulate her on a new teaching position she had just been assigned. Having lost her husband to cancer four years before, she knew the pain he was feeling, and offered her condolences. As they talked their connection grew, so they talked a little longer. Soon the church was silent and the parking lot was empty. They went for coffee at a nearby restaurant and ended up talking right through to the dinner hour. By the time *they parted, Doug says he knew that he had been sent an angel to help him heal and to restore his faith that he could love again. Less than a year later they were married. To this day, they both still call their meeting a miracle of love.*

It's interesting how miracles often happen when we act in good faith, reach out to others, and open ourselves up to kindness that is offered. When was the last time you opened up and asked for something that you wanted...not hinted, implied, or wished, but actually asked? It is quite possible that you are not even sure of what it is that you want.

On the other hand, you are probably quite sure about what you don't want. For instance, at work you may know that you don't want any more sales responsibilities or any more international travel. At home, you may know that you don't want any more chauffeuring assignments and you don't want to do grocery shopping anymore. Also, you may be perfectly clear that what you don't want for your birthday is a dinner out with your in-laws.

Most of us do pretty well with identifying what we don't want. The problem is that being specific about what you *don't* want, only limits the field of possibilities to about one million minus one. With this approach, the probability of receiving what you want is quite low. The key to satisfying relationships is communicating what you *do* want.

Hear that cheering crowd in the background? That's a huddle of husbands responding to that last statement. It is generally true that men seem to ask for what they want more often than women do. We women seem to appreciate something more if we didn't ask for it. It isn't that we value mind reading, exactly. It's that we may have been taught that it's not nice to ask for things. Or we may believe that if people really pay attention and get to know us, they will know what we want without needing a list. The problem is, if you haven't expressed such preferences, how is your significant other to know?

The same is true with work relationships or professional partnerships. If you are not sure what role you'd like to assume, or what "rewards" would be most meaningful, or what kind of agreement is most comfortable for you, how can you negotiate? Believe it or not, most of your clients, coworkers, and partners do not stay up all night trying to figure out how to annoy and disappoint you. It is much more probable that they just don't know how to satisfy you. In Chapter One you were asked to dream about what you would like in your relationships. One way to turn that dream into a reality is to let others in on your dream. Communicate what is most important to you, what makes you comfortable, what challenges you, what delights you, what energizes you, what helps you do your best work, what kind of support you need when you're under pressure, and what behaviors enhance your trust.

To receive graciously is to stop and give thanks for all the love that is offered us by showing respect, recognition and gratitude. Such gifts are always appreciated and cost so little. Consider those who have been important contributors to your life and try telling them what they mean to you (in a prayer or a journal entry if they have passed on). Thank them for the gifts they have brought into your life, and let them know how they have helped you to grow.

Consider a phone call, a note, or even a prayer. When you have time to prepare, you could even create a validation box for someone you love by filling a lovely keepsake container with handwritten messages of appreciation...one for each trait or special moment that you are grateful for. It's not unlike presenting a box of fortune cookies, except the messages are of personal affirmation rather than predictions. One year I created such a box for my sister and invited her husband, sons, and friends to add their own messages. You might also consider writing a letter of tribute as Doug did for his brother Bill.

Bill was battling leukemia when he received a beautiful letter from his younger brother. In the letter

Doug eloquently expressed the many things that he had learned from Bill and described the traits that he so admired. He spoke of Bill's quiet inspiration and how he had shown so many the power of courage and unconditional love. The loving tribute meant so much to Bill that he had it framed and hung on his living room wall within 24 hours. Later, when Bill's battle with cancer was lost, Doug was asked to read that letter at Bill's funeral. With dignity, poise, and great affection, Doug delivered a touching testimonial that was a rare gift for all of us who attended. It soothes the wounded soul to be in the presence of such generous love. The next Christmas Bill's eldest daughter had the letter reproduced and beautifully framed for those closest to her father. A sincere letter intended to honor one, turned into a gift for many...first for Bill, then his friends, and for his entire family.

You might even think about recording your note of appreciation, stating all of the things that you love and admire about someone dear to you. That way, even when you are not around, the sound of your voice will resonate with love in someone's heart. Last Christmas I created such a tape for my husband, Mike, recording all the things that I admire about him and expressing gratitude for the great love he brings into my life. I wanted him to hear my spoken words of affection even when we are apart.

Taking the time to say thank you is such a generous expression of affection. In this age of electronic mail and answering machines, a simple live phone call or brief visit may be the most precious gift of all. Recently a busy friend of mine (who is undeniably the queen of thoughtful gifts and personal recognition) took two hours out of her very hectic schedule to help me with some research. She was thoughtful, articulate, and made an enormous contribution. But she wrapped this most generous gift with an elegant ribbon...a heartfelt expression of what our friendship means to her.

In the writing of this book, another friend sent a gift of thanks. He had reviewed an early draft to provide feedback for strengthening the manuscript and along with his insightful comments, he sent this heart-brightening message: "You've always been there for me, listening, coaching, helping sort things out and providing perspective. I don't know if I've ever REALLY said thanks for the last 20 years or so but wanted to say it here. And now, a new perspective and plan for truly discovering the best half of our lives! You are brave, amazing and truly one of a kind."

Treasures such as these are carried very close to the heart. How would you enjoy expressing your sentiments to those you would like to "celebrate"...a hand-written note, a surprise phone call, or perhaps even a videotape?

WORK FOR CONSTANCY

Perhaps the most essential element of building strong relationships is trust. Whenever I am asked to facilitate a team building retreat or mediate a conflict between two parties, the first thing I assess is the level of trust. Do people trust that they won't be hurt? Do they trust that others will back them up? Do they trust that what is said is true? Do they trust that everyone's goal is to be fair? If trust is low, there will be little synergy; connections will be weak and intermittent. But we can strengthen connections, by consistently behaving in a trustworthy fashion.

One way to build trust in relationships is to *assume positive intent*. That is, don't assume that there is a self-serving motive behind a positive behavior, or an intent to harm behind what you perceive as a negative behavior. How many times have you heard someone say, "Oh, right...he's just doing that so he'll look good...or because she wants something...or to protect his backside?" Perhaps you have even found yourself mentally responding to a compliment or kind gesture with, "I wonder what he wants?" Have you ever confronted someone with great indignation about a personal affront only to find out that it was completely unintended? Such skepticism is often the catalyst for a landslide of false interpretations, hurt feelings, and—eventually—broken bridges.

A second way to build trust is to *be emotionally honest*. If you have a problem with a significant other, business associate, or partner in a cause, take it up with your partner—not with others—first. If you are unsure of something and need time to think it over, let your partner know. If you have already forgiven a "relationship slip," then let it go, don't mention it...now or later. Forgive and let go or resolve and let go. Either way, try to stay current in the relationship.

A third way to build trust is to *be open yourself*. Allow close partners to see a little vulnerability and frailness. If you're afraid, worried, or confused...let those close to you know. How else can they support you? If you mess up, say so. If you make mistakes, take responsibility. When you let others into your imperfect—and entirely human—world, you create a connection that says "I'm like you" and "I trust you enough to let you see the real me...warts and all."

Finally, to build trust you must *keep commitments*. We trust those who do as they say, people we can count on. If you say you'll meet at eight, be there. If you offer to handle an account, do it. If you promise to go dancing, dance. We deepen or weaken connections one act at a time, so every day you have a choice. You can choose to strengthen your relationships or let them weaken a bit.

If you believe it would be satisfying to have deeper connections in your life, decide today which relationships need work and which relationship-enhancing behaviors you need to work on. If you're not sure how to enhance your relationships, begin by testing yourself on how well you know the other party or parties. Do you know what they value most? Have you ever discussed what behaviors they consider trust building and which behaviors they consider trust busting? Do you even know personal preferences, such as what little gifts delight them, when they most enjoy communicating, or what it is that puts distance between you?

Consider asking what you can do to provide support. Then, make a commitment to make building bridges a priority in your life. Replacing a board now and then is easy, but if you wait until the foundation starts giving way, you'll have to start all over again. ⌇

CHAPTER *6*

stretch until you feel it

move out of your comfort zone
to realize your potential

BEYOND FAMILIAR...

JUST PAST FEAR...

THAT'S WHERE LIFE EXPANDS.

S. W. Z.

CHAPTER *6*

stretch until
you feel it

*t*he Swahili word "utoto" stands for energy, youth, and newness. In midlife, we often seek utoto, intuitively wanting to extend life and resist degeneration. The principle of entropy is defined in Webster's dictionary as "the degradation of all matter and energy in the universe to an ultimate state of inert uniformity." In other words, all things—including human beings—will eventually break down, if there is no change. However, unlike inanimate objects, human beings can interact with the environment in a cyclical way that either accelerates or inhibits our decline. We have an opportunity to act and learn, thereby growing to a new level where we can act and learn again, and then advance to yet another level. If we learn and grow, we evolve. If we don't, we decline. Although we often hear references to just "coasting" or maintaining the status quo, there actually is no status quo. If we do nothing, our system will not stay the same...it will deteriorate. In effect, there are only two modes of energy utilization available to us: expansion or contraction.

Fortunately, the benefits of change—feeling young and alive—often outweigh the costs. So we risk pride, income, and comfort in pursuit of continuous growth and adventures large and small. When we do, we are generously rewarded with renewed energy that only comes from living fully. People who seem younger than their years often make learning a lifetime adventure. They read, take courses, and converse with people about all sorts of things. They may attempt new physical challenges such as aerobics, weight training, or even tap dancing, or become thrill-seekers, trying their hand at skydiving, mountain climbing, or scuba diving. Some find new ways to be of service, while others delve deeper into spiritual matters.

We can choose to continuously improve mind, body, and spirit or we can choose the path of decline. We can interact with the universe in an exchange of energy, or we can block renewal of our system and simply let our batteries wear down. A generation ago, our parents looked forward to retiring at about age 65 and spending a few more years winding down. Today, most midlifers will have the opportunity for new adventures, physical mastery, and deepened self-awareness and spirituality. The question is: "Will we choose to accept the opportunity and expand ourselves, or will we turn from the opportunity and contract?" The choice is ours. Lou, a Philadelphia corporate executive, chose to stretch...literally.

Lou is a likeable, talented, high-energy corporate executive with a career that spans two continents. A few years ago, his body started signaling that his fast-paced lifestyle was taking its toll. Although everyone was telling him to relax, slow down, and reduce his stress level, he denied there was a problem. "It's just my personality. I'm a high-energy guy," he'd say. "I love this pace...really." It's hard to argue with Lou; he's very convincing. But when a parade of ailments began—sinus infections, heart irregularities, and chronic stomach trouble—it was becoming more apparent that something had to give. He knew it, but it took a while to admit it.

Lou is from the school of "never let them see you cry," so while he was dealing with these personal problems, he still put in 12- to 16-hour days and went nonstop seven days a week. He was on a "busy-is-better" treadmill and wasn't sure how to get off.

In his mid-forties, he has already achieved great career success and has many interests. He travels often and is a gourmet cook and a gadget buff. He always goes the extra mile for others and looks like energy in motion most of the time. Although everyone kept telling him to relax, it was not sinking in. It was like telling a caged lion not to pace. The tension of wanting out was mounting, but he was in strange territory. He'd always been competent in the career domain, but this was about personal mastery.

Convinced he was too young to burn out, he started working out, eating better, and moderating his work schedule. But it was not easy. Lou has always loved good food and been passionate about his work. He's never been particularly fond of exercise, or anything routine. Always looking for something new, he'd start a regimen, stop and then start over again. Then he asked a trainer in the company gym to be his fitness coach. "That," says Lou, "made all the difference." The executive who had been a cheerleader all of his life—encour-

aging others to go for the gold, guiding employees to new levels of performance, and boosting spirits when the going got rough —now had a cheerleader of his own.

Today, he's 25 pounds lighter and feels—in his own words—"the best I've felt in 20 years." The people who work with him say he's like a different person; he delegates more and maintains a better personal/professional balance. He even rekindled an old passion by buying into and now regularly flying a private plane. Being master of your own fate does not mean doing everything alone. It often means securing the support you need to achieve professional and personal well-being.

Midlife stretching often occurs in one of the three major areas of mind, body, or spirit. Some midlifers go forward on all three fronts at once, while others take a more sequential approach.

BRAIN AGILITY

Perhaps you have heard the aphorism, "Use it or lose it." The truth in that saying becomes abundantly clear when somewhere in our late forties we start to forget things. At first it may seem humorous...or maybe we just use humor to help us cope. "Gosh, I went to introduce my best friend the other day and I couldn't remember her last name." Nervously, we all laugh. "I know, I know," we say, "I can't remember my own name some days." The truth is, the research on age-related mental functioning is quite heartening. While we might experience a slight lessening of short-term memory, we do not actually *lose* brain cells in the large numbers we formerly thought. Instead, it seems that brain cells go dormant from a lack of stimulation and challenge. So, once again: use it or lose it. It is good news that we can actually grow new dendrites, or connectors to transmit messages across the network of our brain.

Every new activity you attempt, every new crossword puzzle you complete, every new piece of information that you learn will help you to maintain brainpower. The more you read, problem-solve, and increase your vocabulary, the more you will give your brain the workout it needs to stay alert. Talk with smart people, enroll in challenging courses, and read about topics that will expand your horizons. Attempt new physical feats, and listen to music that you normally don't hear. Travel, learn a foreign language, and immerse yourself in different cultures. You are in charge of the contraction or expansion of your brain functioning as you prepare for your second adulthood. You can risk and stretch and challenge yourself or you can play it safe, rest on your laurels, and comfort yourself. If you want to be mentally sharp for the rest of your life, put your brain on the same kind of fitness regimen you would require for a champion racehorse that you were preparing for the Kentucky Derby: feed it, exercise it, and challenge it.

BODY STRENGTH

So much has been reported on the benefits of a healthy body that you would think we would all be eating well, exercising regularly, and managing life stresses beautifully. Surely it is not from a lack of information that we overindulge, underexercise, and allow stress to take its toll. Instead it must be related to inertia. We get on a roll, learn habits that are hard to break, and just keep going unless we receive some sort of wake-up call...a heart attack, loss of a peer, loss of physical strength, or even jeans that no longer fit.

However, we don't have to wait for a flashing neon sign; we can be proactive. We don't wait until the engine of a car seizes up before adding oil. We don't wait until we have a mouthful of cavities before brushing our teeth. We don't wait until a houseplant is shriveled before adding water (okay, some of us do...but you get the point). We already know the habit of maintaining top performance...we just don't always apply it to our bodies. As with changing any habit, half the battle is won with intent and half with persistence.

It is often said that whatever you pay attention to in your life will become larger, and whatever you ignore will diminish. Direct energy at something, and it grows. Withdraw energy from something, and it withers. You know this intuitively. When a child has a hurt, we try to distract him; with older children we say, "Try to focus on something else." When a friend talks of all the things that can go wrong with an upcoming presentation, we say, "Don't even imagine that" or "Don't put that out there." Successes are not born out of fear or from negative focus, but out of the power of strong intent. We receive what we desire by imagining what we want and knowing why we want it. Ask any sports coach which contemplation is more empowering for their team: envisioning what they don't want (fumbles) or imagining what they do want (well-executed plays). Winners focus on what they do want.

Jane is a 47-year-old teacher who had been gaining weight steadily for some time. This past year she lost 75 pounds. In describing how she did it, she talked of her resolve to be fit by the time she and her husband escaped on vacation from the wintry Northeast to warm island breezes. As she spoke it was apparent that her will had been very strong and her intent perfectly clear. She had picked out specific clothes to wear and held onto an image of how she would look in them. Her goals were clear: when she lost the weight her rewards would be a fit body, increased energy, and a hard-earned vacation.

If you want to manage your weight, try paying attention to the "fit" you. Repeat positive affirmations many times during the day, saying such things as: *"I am just the right weight for me"* or *"I eat what my body needs"* or *"I'm in great shape."* If a what-you-don't-want thought (*"I'm soooo fat...lazy...weak, etc."*) pops into your head, just evict it. Say right out loud: "That was up until now. Now, I am fit...fine...in charge, etc."

Visually imagine pictures of your svelte self (or exercising, veggie-eating, meditating self) on your refrigerator, morning mirror, and daily calendar. If you have no picture of your intended self, paste a headshot of you on a magazine photo of a walker, tennis player, or other fitness role model. When you close your eyes at night, accept who you are and imagine who you want to be.

Make your intent specific and demonstrate your commitment by writing and posting positive intent fitness goals such as: *"I am at my ideal weight at Christmas,"* *"I'm running a five-minute mile in June,"* or *"My cholesterol is normal next check-up."* Remember to phrase all intent statements in the positive. Reinforce what you do want, such as ideal weight or completing a five-minute mile. You will simply increase attention to what you don't want if your goals are phrased in the negative, such as *"I won't be overweight,"* or *"I won't be sedentary."* Also, remember to use present-tense verbs when you phrase your fitness goals and affirmations: *"I am full of energy"* instead of *"I will be full of energy."*

Positive intent's partner in strengthening your body is persistence. As with any goals, if you want to *be* different, you've got to *do* different...every day. It takes persistence to make transitions. Old habits die hard, and most of us are not able to make major changes in one attempt. It is more likely that we will succeed in shifting mindsets, then images, and then one behavior at a time. We might succeed in the short run, experience a setback, and then get back on track. So "chunk" your body-strengthening goals into smaller "sub-goals" with shorter deadlines. As you reach each one, you'll be inspired to move on to the next, and if you should have a setback, you'll be able to fall back on all the previous small successes to keep you hopeful.

Be patient and forgiving of any slip. Acknowledge it, forgive it, and move on. There is no need to give up on a whole goal (bench-press 50 pounds by January) because you missed one sub-goal (lift weights three times this week). I'm sure that you have run into a pothole or two in your travels. They give you a jolt, but they seldom derail you. The happiest people I know all demonstrate a commitment to do whatever it takes. They don't "take a stab" at happiness or "give it a try." They decide. If your desire is great and your intent is clear, you are unstoppable.

A spunky female friend of mine took up golf at the age of 47. In six months she was playing better than her husband was...and he had been playing golf for most of his adult life. She was determined—and disciplined— and proved that it's never too late to learn if you are willing to do what it takes. She could have convinced herself that her husband had too much of a lead, and that she would never be able to play at his level. Or she could have stopped trying when she reached his level. But she didn't. In midlife, she embarked on a whole new adventure and quickly rose to the top. Within two years, she was winning tournaments, chairing leagues, and improving her handicap every month. She's happy and looks half her age. Stretching is good for us...and so is having a passion.

WISDOM OF THE SOUL

Often at midlife there is a natural leaning in the direction of spirituality. As we face our own mortality, we glance back at the first half of our lives and ask many questions. Has it been worth it? What have I learned? Have I focused on the important things? Have I become who I want to be? Have I made a difference? Where have I given love?

Not only do we question the path we've taken; most of us look for stronger connections. We seek deeper friendships and more intimacy with loved ones. Many of us establish or strengthen relationships with nature, God, and our higher selves. We are drawn to larger issues of peace, order, and knowledge of the universe. Often we sense a significant shift in focus from our individual survival to a greater good.

Perspective, purpose, and simple pleasure provide a new rhythm for our forward march. The crossroads between our first and second adulthoods seems to be a perfect spot to pause and catch our breath. This is the place where many of us decide that it is time to veer off the familiar path in pursuit of new adventures. It is time to create a different life...a life that tickles the soul.

To tickle the soul, we've got to get in touch with the soul. Such inner reflection requires more silence than activity, more openness than intent, and more perception than planning. We can increase our self-awareness by developing habits of meditation and inspiration. Set aside a bit of reverie every day...perhaps 15 to 30 minutes at the start of each day and 15 to 30 minutes before you sleep. Find a quiet place where you can be alone and absolutely still. Relax yourself with a little deep breathing and then pose a purpose question (How can I be of service to others?), ask for guidance (What is the way out of this dilemma?), or state your openness to your inner wisdom (I am learning). Ask or state...then just wait. Your awareness will be heightened, and if not immediately, then later when you least expect it, a concept will appear. All you need to know is available to you; practice regular silence so you can hear.

Silence is not the only way to strengthen your spirit; you can also feed it with uplifting music, imaginative thoughts, inspiring prose. Read (or listen to tapes of) life-affirming material. Some of my personal favorites are books by Scott Peck (*The Road Less Traveled*), Jack Canfield and Victor Hansen (*Chicken Soup for the Soul*), Deepak Chopra (*The Seven Spiritual Laws of Success*), Stephen Covey (*The 7 Habits of Highly Effective People*), Wayne Dyer (*You'll See It When You Believe It, Wisdom of the Ages*), and Jim Donovan (*This Is Your Life, Not a Dress Rehearsal*). Listen to music that inspires you and read stories that touch your heart. Interact with people who have a sense of purpose and joy, and who are generous, sharing souls. Visit often the places that inspire you and bring you inner peace. Your favorite might be a wooded area, a deserted beach, your own little garden, or a place of worship.

Developing your spiritual self does not take great effort. In fact, to the contrary—this type of stretching flows naturally when you are all alone, with a still mind and an open heart. As you free yourself from all outside clatter, your inner voice will speak. Words of healing, love, and purpose will provide any guidance that you seek. You won't need to find courage to reinvent your life because you will know intuitively just which path is right.

EVOLUTION OR ENTROPY?

The choice to grow rather than decline involves many conscious choices to expand rather than contract. We forgive or hold anger; we explore or ignore; we give or withhold; we escape or participate. When we expand, we feel alive and when we contract, a piece of us dies.

On my fiftieth birthday I did something that I had wanted to do for a long time. I went hot air ballooning. My husband and brother came along—against their better judgment, in a gesture of love. We all helped the pilot unfold the colorful waves of cloth and fill the balloon with air. Excitement grew as we soared above a patchwork quilt of land and glided to a wondrous place. Beyond familiar...just past fear...that's where life expands.

Mike, an executive vice president of a 200 million dollar bank, dreamed of opening his own advertising agency or design studio someday. While he studied serious painting as an avocation, he never gave up on his dream of striking out on his own. But the successes, security, and the corporate culture of the banking industry were just too comfortable...too familiar...to abandon.

Then in a quirky turn of fate, opportunity knocked. Merger mania hit the financial services industry and the chance to leave...with a parachute...was offered. He took the leap of faith.

He left banking and started his own advertising agency. Within two months, he wished he had done it ten years before. Twelve years later, he employs six people, and has sales approaching one million dollars per year.

Sharing the same entrepreneurial spirit as many of his clients whose products and services he markets, Mike soon investigated an undeveloped niche of great interest...heirloom quality, hand crafted nativities.

Venturing out paid off again. Today, while he runs his advertising agency and builds custom nativity stables, the world's largest nativity manufacturer reproduces his original designs in high quality resins and sells them throughout a network of 5,000 retail locations. Business experience, a passion for the arts, and spirited enthusiasm for conceptualizing ideas came together in a manifestation of potential that required imagination and faith.

Consider for a moment the "peak experiences" of your life...times when you felt exhilarated and completely alive. The times when you dared to do something different and your world grew larger. Perhaps you have met physical challenges such as mountain climbing or skydiving. Or maybe you met someone whom you always wanted to meet, or traveled to a foreign place. Maybe you had an extraordinary insight, feasted on a gorgeous sight, or connected with someone in a rare and powerful way. Write them down, recall how you felt, and savor the experience all over again.

Susan Jeffers writes, in *Feel the Fear and Do It Anyway,* that our fears can be broken down into three levels. She defines Level 1 as "surface fears" which include things that happen such as accidents or loss and things that require action such as public speaking or ending a relationship. Level 2 fears involve "inner states of mind" and include fears such as being conned or rejected. A Level 3 fear, which Jeffers says underlies all other fears, is simply "I can't handle it!" She asks the question, "If you knew you could handle anything that came your way, what would you possibly have to fear?" The answer is "nothing." Jeffers' book (also available on audiotape) is filled with insights, tips, and specific techniques for moving through your fears.

When you take a risk, learn something new, or move into places you haven't known before, your life is never the same. Moving through the fear gives you confidence, and experiencing the joy offers a promise. You know you can and you know it's worth it. ⤺

CHAPTER 7

make a difference every day

change the world
one act at a time

THE ENERGY YOU EXPEND
IN SHARING YOUR GIFTS
COMES BACK TO YOU
MANY TIMES OVER,
BECAUSE YOU ARE DOING
THE WORK OF YOUR SOUL.

S. W. Z.

CHAPTER 7
_____

*make a difference
every day*

*M*ost of us want our lives
to count for something. At the end of our time on earth,
we'd like to be able to say that we made a difference...that
we left a legacy. At midlife, when we begin to accept that
we are not going to live forever, we often start whistling
Peggy Lee's tune, "Is That All There Is?" We'd like to
understand the meaning of life and how we fit into the
"greater plan."

Gail Sheehy writes in *New Passages* that middle-
aged baby boomers report a high sense of well-being in
their early fifties, when we also demonstrate an optimistic
attitude of progress, growth and change. Instead of resign-
ing ourselves to inevitable decline when earlier catalysts
for high life energy diminish (raising children, mastering
careers, honing athletic skills), we find new ways to be
alive. We try to add more meaning to our lives by making
a difference in the world.

In our search for meaning, we look for ways to do what we love, use our unique talents, and make a contribution. That contribution can take many forms. It might be adopting a child, teaching adults, working for a charity, or restoring people's faith. It might be providing jobs, preserving history, or easing the burden of others. It might be caring for elders or mentoring the next generation. It might be creating art, spreading wellness, or improving the quality of life. It might be small acts of kindness or the sharing of lessons learned.

One reason the search for meaning has become more important is that we anticipate living longer and retiring earlier, and cannot imagine "loafing" for a full 20 to 30 years. "A woman who reaches age fifty today—and remains free of cancer and heart disease—can expect to see her ninety-second birthday," Sheehy writes, and "the average healthy man who is 65 today—an age now reached by the majority of the U.S. population—can expect to live until 81." So most of us want to make that additional time useful...as well as enjoyable. We want to do what satisfied people say makes them bounce out of bed each morning: "Do what you love and make a difference every day."

Ann, a gifted actress and mother of two, found herself facing a dearth of meaningful female roles. Opportunities were scarce and understandably, she was anxious. What had been a good livelihood seemed to be slipping from her fingers. But, instead of stewing about her bad luck or the lack of good roles for mature women, she re-applied her special gifts...and fulfilled a lifelong dream in the process.

Without any formal teacher training, she applied for a position as drama consultant at Manhattan East, a middle school that was established to bring together youngsters of all races and economic strata. The innovative school does not require certification for special subject consultants...just exceptional talent. Ann is an extremely gifted teacher who quickly establishes rapport with youngsters and manages short attention spans like a master. She touches hearts, taps potential, and builds self-esteem from the inside out. It is her gift—not a certificate—that distinguishes her.

Soon the part-time drama consulting led to private coaching, and the coaching led to private acting classes. Her schedule is now so full that she works six days a week all year. The word is definitely out. She is recognized for her unique ability to elicit extraordinary work from youngsters with a wide range of backgrounds. But, here is the best part: when Ann was a youngster she always dreamed of running an animal farm for underprivileged children. Recently, after coaching several private scholarship students who had seen their share of tough times, she told me, "Well, I didn't get my farm, but I sure did find my field." Taking charge of her career, she transformed herself from entertainer to teacher and—in the process—realized a lifelong dream. She loves what she does, and she makes a difference every day.

In Chapter One you were asked to define your purpose...how you can use your unique gifts for the benefit of others. You were asked to reflect on your positive personal traits and how you enjoy expressing them. It is the merging of these elements that guides you to do what you love.

However, knowing your life purpose and unique gifts usually will not point you to a specific career or avocation. Instead you become aware of a spectrum of ways that you can use your gifts in the service of others. For instance, I can facilitate growth in a number of ways: as a speaker, seminar leader, consultant, individual coach, or community volunteer. In fact, I *have* facilitated growth by serving in all of those roles.

Once you know your purpose, you can find meaning in a number of ways. But with so many options, you may find your direction a bit fuzzy. To zero in on which application of your unique talents is best for you, try reflecting on a few questions.

1. *What is it that leaves your heart feeling full and your soul at peace?*

2. *What do you do especially well...with incredible ease?*

3. *What are you always interested in learning more about?*

If you are not using your special gifts for the benefit of others, you will feel drained. It takes great effort to deny your truth and do what you don't love...to disconnect from your dreams. While continuing the status quo may seem like the easier path it is both exhausting and futile.

You will seldom feel productive if you're not doing what you love. More likely, you'll feel as though you're running around in circles, but getting nowhere of any consequence. You might also feel disconnected, as though you are just going through the motions but living someone else's life. Perhaps you feel stressed, depressed, or confused and have nagging thoughts that you are headed down the wrong path. Maybe you sense that you have ignored something precious for far too long. Perhaps the reasons behind putting your dream aside (to make more money, please your family, avoid risks, or do the practical thing) just don't seem that compelling anymore.

When you are tapping into your potential and passion, it will become perfectly clear to you... and to everyone around you. People will often say, "You really love what you do, don't you?" Time will seem to fly, but you will not feel anxious or burdened. The energy you expend in sharing your gifts comes back to you many times over, because you are doing the work of your soul.

Paula believes she has the best job in the world at the YMCA...and that her life ranks in the top 10 percent. She was blessed with a magnificent career at AT&T, where she worked for 22 years and learned the best of business skills as well as great appreciation for the importance of focusing on mission and the people who benefit from your mission. As a volunteer throughout her life, her dream was fulfilled when she became the president of the YMCA of Greater New York in 1990. "The

YMCA mission seeks to help people—particularly our

youth—to grow in spirit, mind, and body while develop-

ing our communities," Paula said. Her transition from

AT&T to the YMCA not only provided "the opportunity to

translate business skills to the nonprofit world, but to

match a professional mission with a personal mission of

helping others in this world to have a better life."

Of course, you don't have to change jobs to fulfill
your purpose. I know of one gentleman who determined
that his editing job for a book publisher was a perfect use
of his gifts. But he wanted to do something more, to give
back. So he joined a literacy group that trained him to
teach adults how to read. He volunteered two mornings a
month for tutoring, edited the agency's newsletter four
times a year, and drafted copy for their annual fundraising
brochure. He added meaning to his life by making a difference in the lives of others.

Although we all seek meaning—with increasing
urgency at midlife—we find it in different ways. Not
everyone needs to find meaning in his or her "day job" as
long as one's overall purpose is being pursued. Consider
how many people in the arts drive cabs, wait tables, clean
houses, or walk dogs as a means of sustaining themselves

while they hone their craft, look for the right projects, and move toward their dream of earning a living by touching people's souls. Would they rather be working exclusively at their craft? Probably, but even a work-for-income job has meaning when it enables you to do what you love and keep your dreams alive.

CONTRIBUTE TO CAUSES
THAT ARE MEANINGFUL TO YOU

A recent *Time* magazine article focused on the midlife phenomenon of giving back, recounting the contributions of well-known professionals. When Colin Powell retired as Chairman of the Joint Chiefs of Staff, he founded America's Promise—The Alliance for Youth, an alliance of nonprofit groups to help young people. Tom Osbourne, former football coach at the University of Nebraska, launched a youth mentoring program which pairs his Cornhuskers with 25 school children in a kind of "buddy system" that follows the youngsters from middle school right through high school.

Some people love what they do and make a huge difference at work...creating jobs for thousands, healing people, teaching, keeping people safe...and yet they still want to give outside of work. At fiftysomething, we often hear peers say that they "want to give back." Having learned a good deal and found much of what we sought, we now want to share what we have.

We all know people who volunteer for "business" or "ego" reasons, but I'm referring to the people who get up early on their only Saturday off in a month to help a family rebuild their burnt-out barn or devote four hours every single week to being a Big Sister or a Big Brother. I mean everyday people who maintain their zest for life by working for something outside of themselves...not for personal gain, but for the sheer pleasure of helping someone else. As we focus on being part of something beyond our own little world, we find meaning by connecting to a much larger world...to mankind.

Both my husband and I have served on numerous nonprofit boards, chaired many fundraising campaigns, and volunteered on a variety of organizational committees over the years. We have also provided monetary support to a wide range of causes. In most cases, we have taken away far more than we have given. Knowing that you have made a positive difference, regardless of how small the effort, is very satisfying. It is especially rewarding to support organizations that are mission-driven and in alignment with your personal mission.

You can increase your passion for life and sense of purpose by embracing a cause or effort that is dedicated to making changes in the world that you would desperately like to see. Your energy and passion will surge as you join forces with people from all walks of life to make the world a better place. Why wait? Contribute in a way that is meaningful to you and you will enhance the level of meaning in your life. You will get up in the morning with direction and go to sleep at night more peacefully.

To identify what causes might be particularly meaningful to you, try answering these few questions:

1. *What type of world news story touches you most deeply...violence, disaster, homelessness?*

2. *If you had a windfall to share with a nonprofit group, which organization would be the lucky recipient?*

3. *If you could donate one Saturday a month to work on something meaningful, what would you do with the time?*

4. *If you could change the world tomorrow, what would it look like? Would it be a safer or kinder place? Would everyone be nourished... physically and spiritually? Would there be more beauty and joy? Would there be more order and interdependence?*

Perhaps as you were answering those questions you discovered a dominant theme. Youth, history, art, literacy, healthcare, the elderly, beautification, the environment, or victim's assistance may be just the magnet for attracting your energy. There are so many organizations that make a difference in the quality of life for others; it won't be hard to find one that is aligned with your vision of a better world. There are free medical clinics serving the uninsured, agencies providing meals for shut-ins, and groups such as Habitat for Humanity which provides housing for those who need it and are willing to invest "sweat equity" by working on their own prospective house and on the houses of others in the program.

Whatever gift you give...time, talent, sweat, or money...if it is for a cause you believe in, you are likely to find great satisfaction in knowing that you are making the world a better place, sharing your gifts one small act at a time.

GIVE SOMETHING AWAY EVERY DAY

In midlife, the search for meaning seems to bring with it a deepening interest in one's own spirituality. As we face our own mortality, more of us ask why we are here, what it is that we have learned, and what—if anything—we are meant to complete before our time is up. Many of us seek inner peace and healing through personal reflection, meditation, and prayer. We look back at mistakes and make peace so we can move forward. As we mature, so it seems does our perspective. Suddenly, things that used to matter—office politics, looking good to neighbors, having the most toys, winning small arguments—now seem inconsequential. Things that we have paid less attention to—self-awareness, personal growth, relationships, and songs of the soul—now surface as worthy of our attention. We reconfirm our values and attempt to live in better alignment with our own principles.

Oprah Winfrey, arguably the most powerful woman in entertainment, surely has every reason to feel great joy. She is beautiful, accomplished, and meets all kinds of interesting people. She could "coast" at this time in her career, but instead she has chosen to produce "change-your-life" television. She interviews inspirational guests, introduces life-affirming books, features everyday people who make a difference, and has established an "Angel Network" to expand the power of giving throughout the world. The Angel Network has raised countless dollars for charity and brought thousands of new volunteers into the fold. If you ever doubt how good it feels to give to others, just tune in to *Oprah* some afternoon and see for yourself. Her "Angel Chain" (where people give someone a gift or an act of kindness and ask the recipient to pass it on) has spread like wildfire. When they show clips of the Angel Chain in action, it is impossible not to be touched. It is amazing how much affirmation is transferred in each simple act of kindness.

In fact, the best way to feel love and abundance in your own life is to give it away. If you have ever helped to build a house for a deserving family or read to someone who couldn't read, you know the joy that you receive...

the joy of expressing your higher self. Helping an elderly neighbor with her groceries, leaving a surprise on someone's pillow, nurturing a sick animal back to health, or reading patiently to a young child...these are the simple ways to make a difference every day.

Ralph is a 52-year-old director of international sales for a computer software firm in Pennsylvania. His job takes him all over the world, so Ralph has accumulated a few first class upgrade coupons. On a recent return trip from Tokyo he was waiting to board a plane in Chicago for the last leg of his journey home when he noticed that five nuns were waiting to board the same plane. In a spontaneous act of kindness, Ralph headed to the gate agent to see if he could upgrade the five nuns to first class using his travel coupons. As luck—or divine intervention—would have it, there were five seats available and the nuns were upgraded to first class. The sisters were thrilled, showering Ralph with prayer cards and promises to pray for him. The crew was stunned at the generosity of this quiet gesture by a business man who just wanted to give the nuns a treat, and they were noticeably inspired to make the sisters' premier first class flight a very special one. As word spread among the crew, Ralph became a bit of a celebrity himself. He received notes, kudos, and many pats on the back. Just before landing, the captain sent him a souvenir bottle of wine with a note from the crew acknowledging his thoughtful act of kindness. Everyone loves an angel!

At Christmas each year my husband and I keep up a tradition that we started the first year that we were married. We "adopt" the wish list of children in an underprivileged family, shop for the items and bring them to the parent with wrapping paper and tags so Mom or Dad can have the joy of wrapping and giving the gifts to their children. It is always a highlight of our holiday...the most meaningful gifts are found in the giving.

Many midlifers are working to make a difference every day—in some small way—in the lives of family, friends, and neighbors. The deeds might include giving small gifts, showing concern, encouraging growth, or lending a neighbor a hand. They might be as tangible as a thank-you note or as thoughtful as forgiving a mistake. If you want to feel more alive, give someone something straight from the heart...no strings attached. You might even consider giving it anonymously. The gift can be as simple as good wishes, a compliment, or a positive thought. It might be a letter of thanks, a note of encouragement, or the surprise completion of a simple chore (walking a dog, grocery shopping, cutting a neighbor's grass). It is with such daily habits of kindness, peace, and forgiveness that many of us in midlife find meaning and a richness beyond measure. When you tickle someone else, you tickle your own soul. ➳

EPILOGUE

*along the road
to a tickled soul*

EPILOGUE

along the road
to a tickled soul

$\mathcal{W}$e've examined many ways to reinvent your life in order to find more depth and exhilaration. The journey starts with redefining your purpose and redesigning your dreams. It continues with enhanced self-awareness and a letting go of things that are slowing you down. Progress is made when you take responsibility for your own happiness and take charge of the thoughts you choose to entertain. You'll really begin to soar when you produce more passion by embracing life and strengthen relationships with habits of caring and love. Once you've reached a new altitude, you'll stretch to go beyond because great vitality accompanies expansion. And finally to experience more of the ultimate joy, you'll share your gifts and make a difference every day.

Whether you are reinventing your life because fate has thrown you a curve ball, or you are beginning the journey because you want more out of life, you are likely to cover much of the same terrain. Like most people, you will probably travel a few well-worn paths of denial, awareness, exploration, and doubt before reaching your new destination. It might help to know some landmarks along the way so you can recognize each trail as you come upon it and find support for continuing your journey.

DENIAL

Travelers on the path of denial entertain thoughts such as "This couldn't be happening to me," or "Things are not really that bad." It's easier to ignore signs that it's time for a change (the queasiness in the pit of your stomach, the disquieting notions in your head, the restless sleep, and the joyless days) than to face the discomfort of change. It seems better to live with *known* negatives than to risk possible new negatives that might be even worse. The danger side of change's double-edged sword shines the brightest. Fear of the unknown is so powerful at this stage that strong needs can be suppressed and intuition totally ignored. It's as if we are in shock—unable to see, hear, or feel what's going on around us. On this path, we pretend and profess a lot, trying to convince ourselves of what we suspect may not be true. Denial prevents any adaptive action because we hold on for dear life to ideas like "everything is fine...really...or at least as good as it ever *can* be."

A few years ago, I worked with a group of chemical workers who were preparing for a major conversion of all processes in their plant. In the group there were a few eager beavers who went willingly into the land of high-tech, many who went skeptically, and a few who dug their heels into the sands of resistance. As you might imagine, those stuck in denial were left behind, still mumbling their mantra of "No way—not in my lifetime" while others who learned new skills and prepared for the changes marched forward to success in the new computerized environment.

While the path of denial can provide a safe haven from too much change, it can also make you vulnerable if you stay on the path too long. Imagine that you are walking down some old railroad tracks, with a high-speed locomotive coming your way. You have two choices. You can stay right where you are and deny that the light in the distance is an oncoming freight train (and eventually get run over), or see the light for what it is, get off the tracks, and take another path.

AWARENESS

When you are ready to diverge from the path of denial, you'll probably pull off for a reality check. Here you will weigh in and come to grips with the truth about what is working in your life and what is not. There will be no more pretending that you are totally satisfied with your work, your marriage, or your personal development.

You'll weigh in, fess up to what you're feeling, and then decide what cargo to unload and what new equipment to pick up. As this new awareness blasts holes in the façade of denial, more light will seep in, and other truths will be illuminated. Needs not formerly met will become visible, beliefs not acted upon will come into focus, and the choices you have made will be apparent. With your passion and desires awakened, you will know what you want and you'll forge ahead to the next connecting path...that of exploration.

EXPLORATION

On the explorer's path you may feel as though you are going around in circles. Although you've committed to moving forward, you won't be sure of the quickest route. You may find that one direction seems right at first, but later deposits you right back where you started. While frustrating, these false starts should be expected. After all, this is new territory. Just shore up your courage and check your internal compass by asking, "Is this direction taking me closer to where I want to be?" If it is, keep going. If not, just say "oops," and choose another route. Soon you will be at your destination, with one more divergence possible along the way...on the path of doubt.

DOUBT

The bushes along the path of doubt are of a prick-ly variety. They may snag you from time to time and even scratch at your new determination. This is where you'll see the cost of change and wonder if it's worth it. You'll be tempted to turn back to more familiar ground and avoid letting go of that last tether. You know you're close to the right path now; you can even sense its foreign nature. The prospect is exciting, but you are leery of adjustments you will have to make. The customs will be different, the mindsets a bit askew. You're not so sure you'll be able to cope in such a strange place. But then you see just up ahead, the prickly path gives way to a spacious, paved, and well-lit road. It's marked with a large, clear sign. "This way," it reads, "to a life that tickles your soul." Doubt fades into determination.

TRAVELER'S AID

Many things will help you to continue your progress journey. Remind yourself of your desires by post-ing them in view and reading them several times a day. Buoy your spirits with life-affirming habits such as yoga, meditation, and self-reflection. Eat right, exercise, and schedule regular periods of renewal where you can go to the balcony, survey your life and assess any shifts you'd like to make. Take the time to tickle your soul by loving, learning, and enjoying the real treasures in life.

As you proceed on your journey, you will likely benefit from support along the way. Think of people who will boost your spirits when they lag and provide direction when you need it. Identify those who have gone before you and ask them to share the lessons they have learned. Find someone who will simply listen and send your own thoughts echoing back. Find others who will ask you questions that no one else would ask...questions of survival intended to save you from yourself. Read inspiring material and enroll in skill enhancing workshops (see the "Resources for Development" section).

Before you begin to recreate your life, pack the gear that will see you through such an exciting journey. You'll need provisions that fuel and things that soothe when you occasionally scrape an ankle. Bring a mirror to see yourself clearly and earplugs so you will be able to hear wisdom in the silence. Carry nuggets of past success to remind you of the many hills that you have climbed, and don't forget to bring along a compass calibrated to your own purpose and design. One more thing that you should bring is a flag to plant at each new summit. There you'll rest and watch it wave, and feel good about how far you have come. ⌐

Potentiality

I take the time to look inside;
I hear the wisdom in my heart.
I dream new dreams...release the old;
I live a life that tickles my soul.

S.W.Z.

Resources For Development

Readings

A Course in Miracles™. Farmingdale, NY: Foundation for Inner Peace, 1975.

Benson, H. with Stark, M. *Timeless Healing: The Power and Biology of Belief*. New York, NY: Scribner, 1996.

Bentley, Karen Anne. *Stop Out-of-Control Eating*. Concord, MA: Lovejoy and Lord Publishing, 2000.

Borysenko, Joan. *Guilt Is the Teacher; Love Is the Lesson*. New York, NY: Bantam Books, 1988.

Canfield, J. and Hansen, M. *Chicken Soup for the Soul*. Deerfield Beach, FL: Health Communications, Inc., 1996.

Chopra, Deepak, M.D. *The Seven Spiritual Laws of Success*. San Rafael, CA: Ambler-Allen Publishing, 1994.

_____. *Ageless Body, Timeless Mind*. New York, NY: Harmony Books, 1993.

Cousins, Norman. *Anatomy of an Illness as Perceived by the Patient*. New York, NY: Norton, 1979.

Covey, Stephen R. *The 7 Habits of Highly Effective People*. New York, NY: Simon & Schuster, 1989.

Donovan, Jim. *This Is Your Life, Not a Dress Rehearsal*. Buckingham, PA: Bovan Publishing Group, Inc., 1999.

Dyer, Wayne W. *Wisdom of the Ages*. New York, NY: HarperCollins Publishers, Inc., 1998.

_____. *You'll See It When You Believe It*. New York, NY: W. Morrow, 1989.

Goleman, Daniel. *Emotional Intelligence*. New York, NY: Bantam Books, 1995.

_____. *The Meditative Mind: Varieties of Meditative Experiences.* Los Angeles, CA: Perigee, 1992.

Jeffers, Susan. *Feel the Fear and Do It Anyway.* New York, NY: Fawcett Columbine, 1987.

Peck, Scott M. *The Road Less Traveled.* New York, NY: Bantam Books, 1993.

Sheehy, Gail. *New Passages: Mapping Your Life Across Time.* New York, NY: Random House, Inc., 1995.

Weil, Andrew, M.D. *Spontaneous Healing.* New York, NY: Alfred A. Knopf, Inc., 1995.

Whitfield, Charles L., M.D. *Healing the Child Within.* Deerfield Beach, FL: Health Communications, Inc., 1987.

Young, J. E. and Klosko, J.S. *Reinventing Your Life.* New York, NY: Penguin Books, 1994.

AUDIOCASSETTES

Guilt Is the Teacher; Love Is the Lesson/ seven-tape set of guided meditations by Joan Borysenko (Mind/Body Health Sciences, Inc., Scituate, MA, 02066).

The Seven Spiritual Laws of Success by Deepak Chopra, M.D. (Amber-Allan Publishing, San Rafael, CA, 1-800-227-3900).

Self-Esteem & Peak Performance/six-tape live-lecture set by Jack Canfield (Fred Pryor, 1-800-253-6139).

MEDITATION LEARNING CENTERS

The Chopra Center for Well Being, 7630 Fay Avenue, La Jolla, CA 92037, 1-888-424-6772. *Call for a certified meditation instructor near you.*

The Inner Passage Center, Doylestown, PA, 1-888-484-9484. Gadodd@aol.com. *Well Being Through Meditation*, Gloria A. Dodd, Director.

ORDERING INFORMATION

Create a Life That Tickles Your Soul can be purchased at
your local bookstore, from online booksellers, or by calling
toll-free 1-800-507-2665.

ABOUT THE AUTHOR

*Suzanne Zoglio is a facilitator who assists individuals and
groups in the development of potential. Dr. Zoglio holds an
M.A. in counseling and a Ph.D. in organizational psychology
and is the founder of the Institute for Planning & Development
in Bucks County, PA. She delivers keynote speeches, facilitates
retreats, and leads motivational seminars. For information
on Suzanne's books, scheduled appearances, or published
articles, please visit her website at* **www.tickleyoursoul.com**.

OTHER BOOKS BY SUZANNE ZOGLIO

Teams at Work: 7 Keys to Success
Order toll-free at 1-800-507-2665

Training Program for Teams at Work
Order toll-free at 1-888-370-8807

The Participative Leader
Order toll-free at 1-888-370-8807

BOOK GROUP DISCUSSION GUIDE

This guide is available online from www.tickleyoursoul.com.
*Just click "Books" on the menu bar and then "Discussion
Guide." While you're visiting the website, you might want to
read an interview with the author (click "Author Interview")
or order a free autographed bookplate (Click "Autograph").*

1. How would you describe your response to being physically
tickled? Stimulated...alert...enlivened...engaged...vulnerable...
exhausted...satisfied... other?   What parallels do you see
between being physically tickled and living a life you love?

2. This book has been described as "an interesting blend of
the mystical and practical." What are some examples of the
spiritual/mystical theme running through the book? Which
ideas or activities presented did you find rather practical?

3. Zoglio suggests that five elements critical to satisfaction in
life are authenticity, self-mastery, relationships, growth, and
meaning. From your own personal experience, which of these
elements do you think we need most at age 30? 40? 50? 60+?
What drives our need for greater levels of one element or
another at various adult development stages?

4. The quotation at the beginning of Chapter One reads:
"A great life is born in the soul, grown in the mind, and lived
from the heart." What does "born in the soul" mean to you?
How are the five elements mentioned above affected by what
"grows in your mind?" When the author refers to "living from
the heart," what do you think she means?

5. In the beginning of Chapter Two, the author reviews various life patterns that can sabotage a person's quest for happiness. Take a few moments individually to jot down a life pattern or self-sabotaging behavior that you have observed either in yourself or someone else. What helps to modify the behavior?

6. Zoglio writes that we can "lighten up by letting go"... by forgiving ourselves or others, by releasing old expectations, by completing things that are on our to-do list. Describe a situation when you experienced a surge in energy by forgiving, relinquishing expectations, or completing something. Why do you think these releases have the potential to energize us?

7. In Chapter Three, the author introduces several techniques for maintaining a positive attitude: affirmations, visualization, reframing, solution sleuthing (turning complaints into questions), going to the balcony, feeding your esteem, meditation or prayer. Which, if any, have you successfully applied and how have you "customized" them for yourself? What other tips can you share for maintaining a positive attitude?

8. Zoglio uses a dance analogy in discussing how some people allow themselves to be lifted by the beauty and delights in life while others resist. When you "allow" it, what lifts your spirit, makes you feel loved, and gets your creative juices flowing? What do you sometimes "allow" to block your enjoyment of what is available to you?

9. To love others - it is often said - one must first love oneself. In Chapter Five Zoglio adds, "Then you will seek deep connections instead of attention, and intimacy instead of activity." What behaviors signal to you that someone is looking for a connection rather than just attention, and what behaviors signal a search for intimacy vs. activity?

10. "Beyond familiar...just past fear...that's where life expands." So begins Chapter Six, which discusses the Swahili word "utoto" and the principle in Physics referred to as "entropy." The message here is clearly the importance of viewing oneself as a "work in progress," but learning, risking, and changing all involve facing fears. Consider the differences between these two types of fear: fear of what we might lose if we take a risk and fear of what we might miss if we don't take a risk. How might your stage of life influence what you fear, and how might what you fear influence your stage of life?

11. When the author refers to "what satisfied people say makes them bounce out of bed each morning," she's referring to having a purpose...using what you have been given to make a difference in the lives of others. Who are some of the happiest people you know, and are they applying unique gifts? Do you know an unhappy person who is gifted, but not applying his or her unique gifts? What do you think about the idea of giving away what you most need?

12. In the Epilogue of *Create A Life That Tickles Your Soul*, the author prepares us for four different paths we are likely to travel before making the changes that make life more meaningful:
DENIAL (no need for change),
AWARENESS (acknowledge you want something more),
EXPLORATION (trial and error),
DOUBT (a lack of belief that you can cope).
Can you remember a change that took you down all four paths?

13. Which of the strategies/tips outlined in the book will you use to change your future? How has your attitude about change and its relationship to life satisfaction been affected by reading this book? In what ways has *Create A Life That Tickles Your Soul* left you more comfortable with seeing your self as a "work in progress" and your life as an ever-expanding adventure?

Join the
TICKLE
YOUR
Soul™
Team

Three ways to join our team.

1. Tell us what ideas, activities, stories or quotes were especially meaningful to you; 2. Describe a change that you have made that was inspired by *Create A Life That Tickles Your Soul;* 3. Share what works for you when you want more peace, passion, or purpose.

Send your comments with your name, address, telephone, FAX, or E-mail (for verification and permission) to:

Tickle Your Soul™ Comments
PO Box 1364, Doylestown, PA 18901
or FAX to 215-348-2563
or E-mail to info@tickleyoursoul.com

For a FREE motivational newsletter, visit our website at **www.tickleyoursoul.com.**

On the website you may also download life-expanding articles, read excerpts of books, and check the author's book signing schedule to see when she will be in your area.

You can also request an autographed bookplate for your copy of *Create A Life That Tickles Your Soul* in case you miss a book signing in your area.

Create A Life That Tickles Your Soul makes a great gift! Available in handsome, dust-jacketed hard cover as well as in paperback. Both editions are available in bookstores nationwide, from online booksellers, or by calling 1-800-507-BOOK.